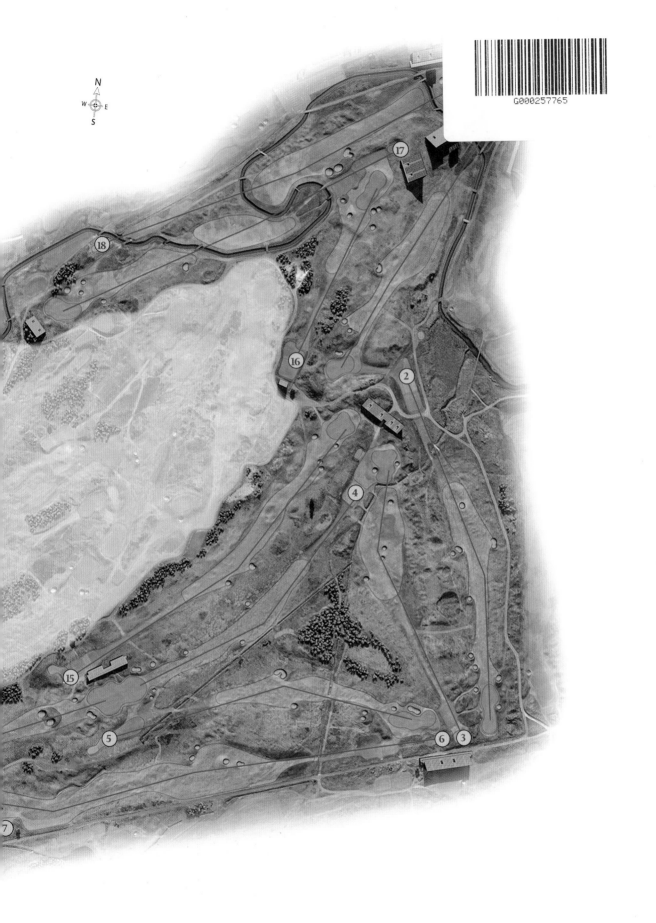

THE
OPEN
147ᵀᴴ CARNOUSTIE

Aurum Press
74-77 White Lion Street, London N1 9PF

Published 2018 by Aurum Press

Copyright 2018 R&A Championships Limited

Course illustration by Strokesaver

Project coordinator: Sarah Wooldridge
Additional thanks to:
NTT Data
Colin Callander
Peter Kollmann

A CIP catalogue record for this book is available
from the British Library

ISBN-13: 978 1 78131 857 7

Designed and produced by Davis Design
Colour retouching by Luciano Retouching Services, Inc.
Printed in Italy by L.E.G.O.

THE OPEN
147TH CARNOUSTIE

EDITOR
Andy Farrell

WRITERS AND PHOTOGRAPHERS

Writers	The R&A	Getty Images	Golf Editors
Peter Dixon	Ross Kinnaird	Andrew Redington	Cliff Hawkins
Andy Farrell	Warren Little	Stuart Franklin	Justin Heiman
John Hopkins	Richard Heathcote	Harry How	Richard Martin-Roberts
Lewine Mair	Matt Lewis	Francois Nel	Brendan Kemp
Art Spander	Jan Kruger	Sam Greenwood	Ker Robertson
Alistair Tait	Tom Dulat	David Cannon	Rob Harborne

Foreword

By Francesco Molinari

What an incredible week it was. I think my first reaction was disbelief, to see my name on the Claret Jug with the best golfers in history, knowing it is engraved on there forever.

To become the first major champion from Italy on this testing course which has beaten me up in the past, going bogey-free on the weekend and playing alongside a great sportsman in Tiger Woods made it even more special. As for being the first *Campione Golfista dell'Anno*, actually I think it sounds even better in English, "Champion Golfer of the Year". *Perfetto!*

There are a lot of people to thank, especially my wife and family for the support they give me when I travel around the world. Each of my coaches has been a massive part of the journey to get here and then there is the Spanish part of the team, my caddie and manager. But also thanks to The R&A and the amazing job by the greenkeepers — the golf course was incredible. To the volunteers and fans, The Open truly is the best atmosphere in golf because of you.

I hope a lot of young kids were watching and will be inspired as I was when I watched Costantino Rocca at St Andrews in 1995. Costantino still is and always will be my hero and my idol. He came so close, now I feel a part of this win was for him.

This year I felt ready for the challenge even if I did not know I would claim our greatest prize. Next year we return to Royal Portrush and I am sure it will be another great Open. Hopefully, by then, it will have sunk in and I will realise what I did at Carnoustie.

The R&A
Championship Committee
– Professional Events

CHAIRMAN
Clive T Brown

COMMITTEE
Will Bailey
John Clark
Pat Crowson
Paul McKellar
David Meacher
Anne O'Sullivan

CHIEF EXECUTIVE
Martin Slumbers

EXECUTIVE DIRECTOR – CHAMPIONSHIPS
Johnnie Cole-Hamilton

EXECUTIVE DIRECTOR – GOVERNANCE
David Rickman

Introduction

By Clive T Brown,
Chairman of The R&A Championship Committee
– Professional Events

The 147th Open at Carnoustie will be remembered for an enthralling and captivating final round in which Francesco Molinari emerged from the chasing pack to win the Championship by two shots and be crowned the Champion Golfer of the Year for the first time.

On his way to lifting the famous Claret Jug, he resisted challenges from Tiger Woods, Rory McIlroy, Justin Rose and defending Champion Jordan Spieth to become the first Italian golfer to win a major championship.

I would like to congratulate Sam Locke, of Scotland, who came through Final Qualifying at The Renaissance Club to take his place in the starting field and win the Silver Medal as the leading amateur golfer.

A crowd of over 172,000, including 25,000 fans under the age of 25, were gripped by events at Carnoustie, setting an attendance record for the famous Angus links. This was 15,000 more than the previous best of 157,000 set in 1999. I would like to thank everyone who came along to Carnoustie for making it a very special Championship.

The Open is highly regarded as a world-class sporting event and there are so many people who deserve a great deal of praise and recognition for delivering the Championship to such a high standard. I wish to thank the members and staff of Carnoustie Golf Links and the thousands of volunteers who worked tirelessly before and during the Championship to ensure its smooth running.

We now look forward to The 148th Open at Royal Portrush, which will be played there for only the second time in the history of the Championship. It will be a pleasure to welcome fans to the famous links for the first time since it last staged The Open in 1951.

Shota Akiyoshi

Min Chel Choi

Lucas Herbert

Sung Kang

147TH CARNOUSTIE

USA

Quicken Loans National	28 June-1 July
Ryan Armour, USA	
Sung Kang, Korea	
Abraham Ancer, Mexico	
Bronson Burgoon, USA	

A Military Tribute at	5-8 July
The Greenbrier	
Kelly Kraft, USA	
Jason Kokrak, USA	
Brandt Snedeker, USA	
Austin Cook, USA	

John Deere Classic	12-15 July
Michael Kim, USA	

THE
OPEN
QUALIFYING SERIES

SOUTH AFRICA

Joburg Open	7-10 Dec 2017
Shubhankar Sharma, India	
Erik van Rooyen, South Africa	
Shaun Norris, South Africa	

Michael Kim   *Russell Knox*   *Haraldur Magnus*   *Erik van Rooyen*

EUROPE

HNA Open de France   28 June-1 July
Julian Suri, USA
Russell Knox, Scotland
Marcus Kinhult, Sweden

Dubai Duty Free Irish Open   5-8 July
Ryan Fox, New Zealand
Andy Sullivan, England
Zander Lombard, South Africa

**Aberdeen Standard Investments
Scottish Open**   12-15 July
Brandon Stone, South Africa
Eddie Pepperell, England
Jens Dantorp, Sweden

FINAL QUALIFYING

Notts (Hollinwell)   3 July
Ash Turner, England
Oliver Wilson, England
Rhys Enoch, Wales

Prince's   3 July
Tom Lewis, England
Haraldur Magnus, Iceland
Retief Goosen, South Africa

St Annes Old Links   3 July
James Robinson, England
Marcus Armitage, England
Jack Senior, England

The Renaissance Club   3 July
Sam Locke[a], Scotland
Grant Forrest, Scotland
Thomas Curtis, England

[a] Denotes amateur

KOREA

KOLON Korea Open   21-24 June
Min Chel Choi, Korea
Sang Hyun Park, Korea

JAPAN

Gateway to The Open   24-27 May
Mizuno Open
Shota Akiyoshi, Japan
Masahiro Kawamura, Japan
Michael Hendry, New Zealand
Masanori Kobayashi, Japan

SINGAPORE

SMBC Singapore Open   18-21 Jan
Jazz Janewattananond, Thailand
Danthai Boonma, Thailand
Sean Crocker, USA
Lucas Herbert, Australia

AUSTRALIA

Emirates Australian Open   23-26 Nov 2017
Cameron Davis, Australia
Jonas Blixt, Sweden
Matt Jones, Australia

EXEMPT COMPETITORS

Dustin Johnson

Phil Mickelson

Jon Rahm

Name, Country	Category
Byeong Hun An, Korea	4
Kiradech Aphibarnrat, Thailand	4,5
Daniel Berger, USA	4,12,15
Alexander Björk, Sweden	7
Keegan Bradley[r], USA	4
Rafa Cabrera Bello, Spain	3,4,5
Mark Calcavecchia, USA	1
Jorge Campillo, Spain	7
Patrick Cantlay, USA	4,12
Paul Casey, England	4,12
Kevin Chappell, USA	4,12,15
Stewart Cink, USA	1,2
Darren Clarke, Northern Ireland	1,2
George Coetzee, South Africa	18
Nicolas Colsaerts, Belgium	5
Jason Day, Australia	4,10,11,12,15
Bryson DeChambeau, USA	4
Jason Dufner, USA	10,12
Paul Dunne, Rep of Ireland	5
David Duval, USA	1
Ernie Els, South Africa	1,2
Tony Finau, USA	4,12
Ross Fisher, England	4,5
Matthew Fitzpatrick, England	4,5
Tommy Fleetwood, England	4,5
Rickie Fowler, USA	4,12,15
Dylan Frittelli, South Africa	5
Sergio Garcia, Spain	4,5,9,12
Branden Grace, South Africa	3,4,5,15
Gavin Green, Malaysia	16
Emiliano Grillo, Argentina	15
Chesson Hadley, USA	13
Adam Hadwin, Canada	4,12,15
Todd Hamilton, USA	1
Brian Harman, USA	4,12
Padraig Harrington, Rep of Ireland	1,2
Tyrrell Hatton, England	4,5
Russell Henley, USA	12
Charley Hoffman, USA	4,12,15
Nicolai Højgaard[a], Denmark	25
Beau Hossler, USA	4
Charles Howell III, USA	4
Kodai Ichihara, Japan	21
Yuta Ikeda, Japan	19
Scott Jamieson, Scotland	5
Dustin Johnson, USA	4,8,12,15
Zach Johnson, USA	1,2
Martin Kaymer, Germany	8
Si Woo Kim, Korea	4,11,15
Kevin Kisner, USA	4,12,15
Patton Kizzire, USA	13
Satoshi Kodaira, Japan	4,20
Brooks Koepka, USA	3,4,8,12,15
Matt Kuchar, USA	3,4,12,15
Anirban Lahiri, India	15
Andrew Landry[r], USA	4
Bernhard Langer, Germany	22

Name, Country	Category
Tom Lehman, USA	1
Marc Leishman, Australia	3,4,12,15
Alex Levy, France	4,5
Haotong Li, China	3,4,5
Yuxin Lin[a], China	27
Luke List, USA	13
Shane Lowry, Rep of Ireland	5
Sandy Lyle, Scotland	1
Hideki Matsuyama, Japan	4,12,15
Rory McIlroy, Northern Ireland	1,2,3,4,5,10
Phil Mickelson, USA	1,2,4,15
Yusaku Miyazato, Japan	20
Francesco Molinari, Italy	4,5,6
Ryan Moore[r], USA	4
Kevin Na, USA	4
Alex Noren, Sweden	3,4,5,6
Thorbjørn Olesen, Denmark	5
Louis Oosthuizen, South Africa	1,2,4,15
Pat Perez, USA	4,12
Thomas Pieters, Belgium	5
Ian Poulter, England	4
Jon Rahm, Spain	4,5,12
Chez Reavie, USA	4
Jovan Rebula[a], South Africa	23
Patrick Reed, USA	4,9,12,15
Justin Rose, England	4,5,12
Brett Rumford, Australia	17
Xander Schauffele, USA	4,12
Brady Schnell, USA	14
Charl Schwartzel, South Africa	4,5,15
Adam Scott, Australia	15
Webb Simpson, USA	4,11,12
Cameron Smith, Australia	4
Jordan Smith, England	5
Matthew Southgate, England	3
Jordan Spieth, USA	1,2,3,4,8,9,12,15
Kyle Stanley, USA	4,12
Brendan Steele, USA	4
Henrik Stenson, Sweden	1,2,4,5
Hideto Tanihara, Japan	5
Justin Thomas, USA	4,10,12,15
Ryuko Tokimatsu, Japan	21
Peter Uihlein, USA	5
Jhonattan Vegas, Venezuela	12,15
Jimmy Walker, USA	10
Matt Wallace, England	7
Bubba Watson, USA	4,9
Lee Westwood, England	5
Danny Willett, England	9
Chris Wood, England	6
Gary Woodland, USA	4,12
Tiger Woods, USA	1
Fabrizio Zanotti, Paraguay	5

(a) Denotes amateur   (r) Denotes reserve

Chris Wood

Champion Golfer Gary Player autographs prints celebrating his 1968 victory.

KEY TO EXEMPTIONS FROM THE OPEN QUALIFYING SERIES

Exemptions for 2018 were granted to the following:

(1) The Open Champions aged 60 or under on 22 July 2018.

(2) The Open Champions for 2008-2017.

(3) First 10 and anyone tying for 10th place in The 146th Open Championship (2017) at Royal Birkdale.

(4) The first 50 players on the Official World Golf Ranking for Week 21, 2018, with additional players and reserves drawn from the highest ranked non-exempt players in the weeks prior to The Open.

(5) First 30 in the Race to Dubai Rankings for 2017.

(6) The BMW PGA Championship winners for 2016-2018.

(7) First 5 European Tour members and any European Tour members tying for 5th place, not otherwise exempt, in the top 20 of the Race to Dubai Rankings on completion of the 2018 BMW International Open.

(8) The US Open Champions for 2014-2018.

(9) The Masters Tournament Champions for 2014-2018.

(10) The PGA Champions for 2013-2017.

(11) THE PLAYERS Champions for 2016-2018.

(12) The top 30 players from the 2017 FedExCup points list.

(13) First 5 PGA TOUR members and any PGA TOUR members tying for 5th place, not exempt in the top 20 of the PGA TOUR FedExCup Points List for 2018 on completion of the 2018 Travelers Championship.

(14) The 112th VISA Open de Argentina 2017 Champion.

(15) Playing members of the 2017 Presidents Cup Teams.

(16) First and anyone tying for 1st place on the Order of Merit of the Asian Tour for 2017.

(17) First and anyone tying for 1st place on the Order of Merit of the PGA Tour of Australasia for 2017.

(18) First and anyone tying for 1st place on the Order of Merit of the Sunshine Tour for 2017.

(19) The Japan Open Champion for 2017.

(20) First 2 and anyone tying for 2nd place, on the Official Money List of the Japan Golf Tour for 2017.

(21) First 2 and anyone tying for 2nd place, not exempt having applied OQS Japan, in a cumulative money list taken from all official 2018 Japan Golf Tour events up to and including the 2018 Japan Tour Championship.

(22) The Senior Open Champion for 2017.

(23) The Amateur Champion for 2018.

(24) The US Amateur Champion for 2017.

(25) The European Amateur Champion for 2018.

(26) The Mark H McCormack Medal (Men's World Amateur Golf Ranking™) winner for 2017.

(27) The Asia-Pacific Amateur Champion 2017.

Carnoustie Shows Its Fun Side

By Andy Farrell

The setting was familiar but something about The 147th Open was different. This was Carnoustie but not as we knew it.

Baked by the sun, the links appeared almost as yellow as the famous 18th hole leaderboards. The ball was rolling forever.

During a practice round Padraig Harrington drove into the Barry Burn on the 18th. Not into the part that loops around the landing area as he did at The Open in 2007 but, as he did with his third shot on the 72nd hole then, the stretch in front of the green over 450 yards away. A day later Tiger Woods measured a three-iron shot at 333 yards. This was going to be fun.

One person who would have loved it was the late, great Peter Thomson, who died earlier in the year. Thomson had no doubt about the standing of the Championship Links. "In its own right Carnoustie is a great course," he wrote, "in the sense that great things have happened there."

As runner-up to the mighty Ben Hogan at Car-

noustie in 1953, Thomson would know. He went on to claim the Claret Jug five times before returning to the Angus venue in 1968. This time the Australian was dismayed by a set-up he thought was "dull and uninspiring" due to the narrowing of the fairways and letting the rough grow. Instead of allowing for "judgement and clever thinking", such a set-up "robs the game of one of its important aspects — necessity to make a choice.

"If golf is a test of threading one's way down narrow, alley-like avenues of untidy growth," Thomson concluded, "it is hardly a game. It becomes an examination. It demonstrates neither temperament nor thought. It is boring for players and spectators alike."

Although there was nothing boring about the conclusion to The Open of 1999 at Carnoustie, the same essential criticism applied. There may have been an element of making sure the course lived up to its fearsome reputation after a 24-year absence from The Open rota but optimal growing conditions — very wet and warm enough — prevailed that summer. All over Scotland the rough was ferocious. On the opening day no player broke par. "That's the nearest I've come to playing rugby

A swan's eye view of the first tee at Carnoustie.

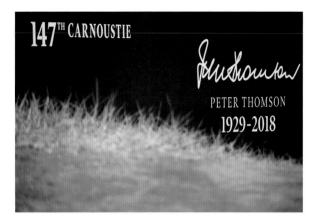

147ᵀᴴ CARNOUSTIE

PETER THOMSON
1929-2018

on a links," said Greg Turner of New Zealand, whose national sport is the 15-a-side game.

That ultimate greenkeeper, Mother Nature, provided something different for 2018. Although the course was under snow in March and the subsequent thaw almost broke the banks of the Barry Burn, two months of sun and an absence of rain produced a very different Carnoustie for this Open.

The fairways dried out and firmed up, while the rough turned straw-coloured and wispy, mostly thin but still tangly in parts. With oasis-like greens, watered to keep them around 10 on the Stimpmeter, the course was never in danger of becoming unplayable. But playing it without thinking was unthinkable.

Here was Thomson's desire for choices made glorious reality. To go long and hope to get lucky with a lie in the rough, or to lay back and face a more exacting approach shot? Or to be indecisive and inevitably end up in a pot bunker?

"The beauty of this course is there's a lot of different ways of playing it but eventually you are going to have to grow up and hit the shots," Harrington explained. "The interesting thing is you can't take all the trouble out. You're going to have to take some risk, skirt by some bunkers. There's no perfect strategy."

Southgate's home away from home

Although Sam Locke, the Scottish Amateur champion, hails from near Paul Lawrie's hometown of Aberdeen, the closest to a local competitor at The 147ᵗʰ Open was Essex's Matthew Southgate.

The European Tour player from Southend-on-Sea used to travel to the Angus venue with his father, Ian, who would play in the popular week-long amateur event called the Craw's Nest Tassie. Ian made friends in the town and became a member of the Carnoustie Golf Club. When Matthew was 10 he attended his first Open at the course in 1999 and returned in 2007. After the son got down to scratch handicap, Ian gave him membership of the club for his 16th birthday.

"I think the whole town know me and my dad,"

Matthew said. "It's like a home away from home. There is not a pub in town where we can't find someone with an old golf story.

"Carnoustie is a completely individual place — I've played golf all around the world and I've never seen anywhere like Carnoustie. It doesn't matter if you're the milkman or a lawyer, as soon as your golf clubs come out, you're all just equal and you're all square on the first tee, let's play golf.

"I must have played 50-odd rounds or thereabouts and watched a couple of Opens here, every day of them. I don't think you can know the course much better than I do." An opening 69 with two eagles proved the highlight of his memorable week.

Three oasis-like greens: the third (top), the 15th (middle) and the first (bottom), with the 16th tee (bottom, right).

Ball-striking prowess would come to the fore, suggested Luke Donald, an interested observer due to injury. His men to watch were Tommy Fleetwood, who produced one of the rounds of the Championship, and Francesco Molinari, who won it. Whatever the condition of the links, precise striking will always be required at Carnoustie.

"A flat, long and extremely exposed stretch of unremitting terrain," was how writer Michael McDonnell described it, "yet therein lies its challenge because Carnoustie requires imagination, invention and determination." Molinari had all three, which put him in good company on the venue's roll of honour.

First came Edinburgh's Tommy Armour, a Scot who became a naturalised American like so many of the pioneers from Carnoustie such as the Smith brothers, Willie, Alex and Macdonald, and Stewart Maiden, who taught the young Bobby Jones in Atlanta. Armour was a hero of World War I who was left blind in one eye but found that was no hindrance to a first-class golfing career which included winning The Open in 1931.

Henry Cotton seemingly took on all-comers in 1937, battling not just the entire American Ryder Cup team but the relentless rain to win the second of three Claret Jugs. Cotton was the greatest British golfer of his time but Hogan was one of the greats of all time. In 1953, he had won the Masters and the US Open and then crossed the Atlantic

Hogan's Alley, the sixth hole, from behind the green.

for his one and only attempt at The Open.

Hogan won by four strokes and could not have got a more enthusiastic reaction had he been playing in his home country. "As the crowd roared its tribute to the greatest golfer most of them had seen or were ever likely to see, Hogan stood quietly, almost humbly so it seemed, and bowed his head in appreciation," wrote Pat Ward-Thomas. "Hogan has said that he was surprised that so many people obviously wanted him to win. At the time he would not realise that the most knowledgeable crowds on earth saw his victory as the only fitting outcome to the Championship and that this transcended all partisan loyalties."

Carnoustie's par-five sixth hole, where out-of-bounds runs down the left and there is a bunker in the middle of the fairway, is called Hogan's Alley in his honour and the myth remains that on the final day, when two rounds were played, his drive in the afternoon finished in the divot from

After returning the Claret Jug, Jordan Spieth discovered during a practice round it is best to avoid Carnoustie's bunkers.

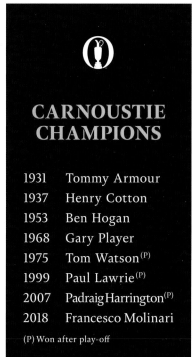

The Barry Burn snaking across the 17th fairway.

his second shot in the morning. Coincidentally, if more prosaically, the late John Jacobs happened to be on the third tee with a view down the sixth hole as Hogan struck his tee shots on both occasions.

"He was the only man in the field who aimed at the tiny gap between the bunker and the out-of-bounds fence," he recalled. "His lightning-quick swing fired the ball off on that line like a bullet, and towards the end of its flight there was just the merest hint of a fade which brought the ball round the back of the bunker and into the middle of the fairway. That was the only way you could knock it on the green in two that day. This was Hogan at his sublime best."

In 1968, Gary Player beat Jack Nicklaus and Bob Charles with the help of a three-wood over the Spectacles bunkers to two feet for an eagle at the 14th hole. Seven years later Tom Watson beat Australia's Jack Newton in a play-off for the first of his five Claret Jugs. Five times Watson played

the long par-three 16th and five times he recorded a four on the card.

Although lack of investment meant the course suffered in terms of conditioning during its hiatus from The Open rota, its absence was more to do with the lack of local amenities. Eventually a new hotel replaced the dilapidated old clubhouse behind the 18th green — and this year a brand new clubhouse opened beside the first tee, providing all necessary facilities for the players.

For all the muttering of the players in 1999, the course still provided a dramatic finale with Jean van de Velde taking a seven at the last and then Paul Lawrie winning the play-off with stunning birdies at the 17th and 18th holes. Lawrie, from Aberdeen, became the first Scot to win The Open in Scotland since Armour.

Another heart-stopping finish occurred in 2007 when Harrington survived those two visits to the Barry Burn on the final hole before defeating Sergio Garcia in yet another play-off.

Diamonds in the rough: Rory McIlroy and his caddie Harry Diamond scouting the links in search of a plan of attack.

Although golf has been played on the banks of the Barry Burn since the 16th century, with Allan Robertson and Old Tom Morris key in establishing its first formal layouts, it was in the mid-1920s when James Braid and others created the course we know today. It was a monster, and with the bunkers, the burns and, given the usual climate on the east coast of Scotland, the rough, no shot could be played without being mindful to both intention and execution. Even before reaching that daunting closing stretch from the 15th in.

Tough but fair, brutal when the wind gets up, a foe to be respected, this is what Carnoustie had become. Fewer visitors might agree with Bernard Darwin's words from an earlier era that the "fine, big, open, sandy seaside course" was "altogether delightful".

Its charm too often remained a Carnoustie secret. But no longer. "This week I saw what a great golf course Carnoustie is," Phil Mickelson declared. "The first few times I played here, I didn't get to see its greatness come through. This week you saw so many different ways to play holes. You saw the nuances and subtleties and just the greatness of this golf course come through.

"It's the first time I've seen that. I thought it was an exceptional Championship."

And so it was. A record attendance for the venue of 172,000 witnessed more great things happen — and it was also a lot of fun.

Paul Lawrie meets participants in The R&A's 9 Hole Championship Final won by Christopher Cudahy and Andrew Sabin.

Champion Golfer Ernie Els with nephew Jovan Rebula, the 2018 Amateur Champion

Junior Open winner Martin Vorster

Presumably, whoever wrote the Wikipedia entry for the Barry Burn was not a golfer. Had the contributor in question known the first thing about the game, they would never have risked referring to so potentially dangerous an enemy as "a minor river in Angus". Minor it is not. As much as any of the contestants, it can dictate who makes off with the Claret Jug when The Open is at Carnoustie.

Ian Poulter, in a sentence as striking as any of the outfits he has favoured across the years, has likened the hazard to "a snake that you have bashed on the head but then recoils to confront you again."

It goes without saying that Jean van de Velde's excursions in and around the water — he ended up with a seven when a six would have served to win him The Open of 1999 — have affected rather more than the player himself. Who, for instance, has played Carnoustie in the last couple of decades and not invoked the Frenchman's name — and probably gone on to think that he or she would have done better never to have mentioned him?

To recap on that day when van de Velde's then wife Brigitte, laughed that she might not cry and van de Velde had to remind the media that the incident was not the mega-tragedy they were making out, the problems began on the 18th tee.

When a wayward drive finished as far afield as the 17th fairway, its owner still had it in mind to finish the Championship in style by knocking a two-iron onto the green. Alas, his ball clattered into a grandstand pole before diving into thick rough. From there he proceeded to chip into the water.

The tide was rising and van de Velde had ever more of a faraway look on his face as he removed shoes and socks and rolled up his trousers in preparation for the next step. Peter Alliss, from the commentary box, was in shock. "Someone kindly stop him," he implored. "Give him a brandy!"

As the ball sank further into the depths, van de Velde did indeed have a change of heart. He took a penalty and knocked what was by then his fifth into a greenside bunker. At which point, he produced a Houdini-like up-and-down to take his place in a play-off where, as everyone knows, he lost out to Paul Lawrie.

Jean van de Velde on TV duty.

It was Craig Boath, today the head greenkeeper but then an apprentice, who set the story in stone. Charged with shoring up the burn's walls in the wake of the Championship, he etched the words "van de Velde 1999" into the cement.

Van de Velde, the best of sports, enjoyed it. In fact, he was happy for his watery exploits to get a mention at the Association of Golf Writers' Annual Dinner on the Tuesday ahead of the 2018 Championship. "Look here," he said humorously, "Paul may have his name on the Claret Jug, but I've got mine on the Barry Burn."

Oddly enough, Padraig Harrington did the double in 2007 of getting his name on the trophy whilst leaving the crowd open-mouthed with his antics on the Barry Burn. He found it off the tee at the 72nd before landing in a further stretch of the water with his third. Telling himself that he was not about "to do a van de Velde", he took a second penalty shot before pinning down the six which resulted in the play-off he won from Sergio Garcia.

You would have to imagine that it was not for old time's sake that Harrington made a return visit to that meandering menace as he amassed one more

six at the 18th in his first round of The 147th Open. Garcia, meantime, began his Championship by catching the burn where it snakes by the 10th green and playing out of the water.

However, the most significant visitor to make a splash on this latest occasion was Kevin Kisner. Seemingly poised to have the halfway lead to himself, Kisner hit his second from the left-hand rough to the underside of the bridge short and right of the 18th green. Though it led to a double-bogey, he was nothing if not philosophical, suggesting that his adventures would make for the best of talking points over dinner.

One way and another, Wikipedia's "minor river" probably featured in as many columns and conversations in 2018 as any of its fellow celebrities including Francesco Molinari, the winner.

Yet of all the stories it has sired, none will ever be up there with van de Velde's. For as long as golf is played, however many names are inscribed on the Claret Jug, Jean is alone in having his distinguished moniker on the walls of that ancient waterway.

Kevin Kisner consults a referee over his drop from the burn at the 18th on Friday.

Kisner Leads in Benign Opening

By Andy Farrell

With barely a breath of wind tickling the links, Sandy Lyle got proceedings at The 147th Open under way and there was a sense of anticipation to go with the quiet calm.

It was not just the feeling that a wide range of players could take possession of the Claret Jug on Sunday evening, but what might occur between 6.35am now and 6.35pm then. How would this baked out Carnoustie links play? How would conditions change over the four days? Indeed, in any particular conditions, how differently would the players approach the task?

There could not have been a more benign morning to open the Championship. The breeze was due to get up in the afternoon but it never reached the strength forecast and 31 players returned scores under the par of 71. This was more than any day of The Open in 2007 and for the entire Championship in 1999.

Kevin Kisner just misses a birdie at the 18th during his 66.

But Sir Michael Bonallack, a former Secretary of The Royal and Ancient Golf Club of St Andrews and the leading amateur in The Open in 1968, had words of warning for Carnoustie days like this. "When the wind is blowing it is probably the toughest course in Britain," he once said. "And even when it is not blowing, it's still the toughest."

After his round, Lyle suggested the "course is up for grabs today," but Tommy Fleetwood's course record of 63 from the Alfred Dunhill Links Championship the previous autumn was never threatened. Instead, the leading score was a 66, five-under-par, from American Kevin Kisner.

"It does not matter what the wind is at all, it's still very hard," said Bernhard Langer, Lyle's fellow 60-year-old. Langer could not remember a firmer links in all his 31 appearances in The Open. "You drop the ball and you can hear it," he said. "It's hard to get the tee in the ground. You have to play really smart, pick your lines and hope you get some good bounces. It's so firm you can't control it. One three-iron goes 240 yards, the next 280. One landed on an upslope, one on a downslope. From the third tee I hit a five-iron trying to be short of the bunker but ended up 20 yards past

Nervous Lyle signs off in style

What could have been more fitting than to have Sandy Lyle hit the opening shot of The 147th Open? The former Champion Golfer had been eligible to play in the oldest of all the major championships since his victory at Royal St George's in 1985, but now, having turned 60, his exemption was in its final year.

This was Lyle's 43rd Open, his 42nd in succession, and he was coming to terms with the fact that it would almost certainly be his last appearance.

Unsurprisingly, he was as jittery standing over his opening shot as he had been as a 16-year-old debutant in 1974. "I was nervous last night, never mind this morning," the Scot admitted afterwards. "I woke up about 1am with one eye on the alarm clock. Then your mind starts thinking about the opening shot and things."

When he arrived on the tee for his 6.35am slot, Lyle jokingly looked at his watch and then at the stand which was full of spectators. "I was hoping I'd maybe get away with 20 people and 15 would probably have been part of my family," he joked.

After splitting the fairway with a four-iron, however, he was up and running. He was one-under-par at the turn but had bunker trouble on the inward half and finished with a 75, four-over-par. The next day, he missed the cut but signed off in true style with a curling birdie putt from around 25 feet at the 18th hole.

What a finish, what a Champion.

A perfect opening day at The Open: Tommy Fleetwood tees off at the first in front of a full house under clear skies.

it. I was left of it, so it was fine, but it's just, you know, tricky."

When Langer, who scored 73, is being outsmarted, you know the examination is far from simple. It made for a fascinating day seeing the different strategies employed by the finest players in the world. Rory McIlroy hit his driver as many times as he felt he could. Brooks Koepka and Thomas Pieters drove the first green. Jon Rahm drove the third green. Others were more cautious, defending Champion Jordan Spieth and the returning Tiger Woods among those to rely on their irons to put themselves in position.

In the second group of the day, South Africa's Erik van Rooyen, who nearly won the Dubai Duty Free Irish Open at Ballyliffin two weeks prior, took the sure and steady approach. "I'm usually a little more conservative, that's my best way round here," he said. "I don't hit a lot of drivers and I get round safely." He birdied the first two holes and got to five-under-par after 15 holes. Ironically, one of the few times he hit a driver off the tee was at

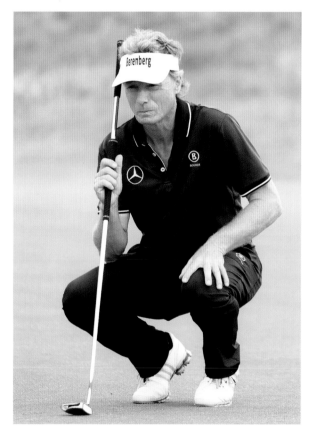

Bernhard Langer tests his wits against the links.

"Rory McIlroy took the high road with his driver and earned the good fortune his gutsy strategy deserved. Tiger Woods took the low road with his 'stinger' iron shots and filled the air with a nostalgic glow."

—Derek Lawrenson,
Daily Mail

"Whatever happens over the rest of his career, young amateur Sam Locke will always have the tale to tell of the afternoon he rolled home a birdie putt on the famous 18th hole at Carnoustie in The Open."

—Eric Nicolson,
The Courier

"Russell Knox admitted playing with Tiger Woods for the first time was awesome — even if he was dreadful. The 33-year-old Scot confessed nerves got the better of him as he traded blows with his hero."

—Robert Martin,
The Sun

"On a day of bridging burns and burning bridges, with the so-called Beast of Angus rendered more a neutered tabby cat, the brave and cautious both attempted to paint sporting comebacks on a bare, brown but sometimes beautiful canvas."

—Rick Broadbent,
The Times

Ryan Moore birdied four of the first six holes on the way to a 68.

the 18th where he found a bunker and ended up making his only bogey of the day.

His score of 67 was soon replaced at the top of the leaderboard by Kisner's 66. The 34-year-old dropped a shot at the fifth but then holed from 40 feet for an eagle at the sixth and from 35 feet for a two at the eighth. His work on the greens was the key to his round as he took only 22 putts, three fewer than anyone else. Three birdies in a row from the 13th and three pars to finish put him out in front.

This was Kisner's fourth appearance in The Open and the only other time he had broken 70 was a 69 in the final round at Royal Birkdale in 2017. But as well as two wins on the PGA TOUR, he lost a play-off for THE PLAYERS Championship in 2015 and in 2017 was leading, or sharing the lead, for the first three rounds of the PGA Championship.

He admitted having to learn how to adapt to links golf but in that regard he had the advantage of growing up and living in Aiken, South Carolina, just over the state border from Augusta, Georgia. Unlike Augusta National which closes for the summer, Kisner's home club of Palmetto stays open through the hottest months, which meant he

Kisner saves par from sand at the 17th after a lesson on playing out of links bunkers from Pete Cowen.

was familiar with the conditions at Carnoustie.

"Palmetto is a great golf course for The Open," he said. "It's firm, fast and undulating around the green. That's why I feel so comfortable here around the greens, because I see the same type of shots at home often.

"The hardest part to get accustomed to is the speed of the greens and I worked really hard on that on Monday. I felt the greens were not as slow as we've had in the past because the wind wasn't up and so the transition wasn't as big a deal.

"It's taken me a few years to understand links golf. I only hit four or five drivers today because I wanted the ball on the fairway. But a few tee balls today landed in the fairway and one-hopped into the rough. Other times the ball is running 50 to 80 yards on certain shots."

Kisner, who was also helped by a lesson on playing out of pot bunkers from English coach

South Africa's Erik van Rooyen birdies the second in his 67.

Korea's Sung Kang returned a two-under-par 69.

Also on 69 was America's Pat Perez.

Pete Cowen at the start of the week, was able to spend the rest of the day at the house he was sharing with a number of other American players and watch everyone else failing to get past his mark.

As a youngster, the Masters was the closest tournament to his home and heart but The Open had a special place in his household. "The coolest thing about The Open growing up was being

Vegas leaves it late after visa handicap

Eager to give himself plenty of time to get over the jet lag and prepare for the challenge of adapting to links golf, Jhonattan Vegas was booked to depart his home in Houston on the Thursday before The Open at Carnoustie. It was only then, however, that the Venezuelan discovered that his visa to enter the UK had expired.

The renewed visa only arrived on Wednesday morning, at which point Vegas flew from Houston to Toronto and then Glasgow, where he jumped on a helicopter, arriving at Carnoustie less than two hours before his tee time for the opening round.

Almost inevitably, his clubs did not make the entire journey, so he needed to cobble together a set from

the equipment companies on site, could only hit 20 balls on the practice range and then, without having seen the course in person, teed-up in The Open for only the second time.

"It took over 14 hours to get here and I had two hours' sleep. So not ideal," Vegas said. "I was actually one-over through eight holes and I was feeling good because the course was really giving me a great feel.

"Then I decided to start hitting the driver and bad things started happening with that shot. It didn't really fit. So I got a few bogeys and shot 76."

A 74 on Friday meant Vegas missed the cut for the second year but returned home with quite a tale to tell.

Eight birdies for American Tony Finau during his 67.

Out in 32, Zander Lombard joined the group on 67.

able to wake early and have it on," Kisner said. "Every other tournament you had to wait until the afternoon. My fondest memories are with my dad watching it and getting to skip church on Sunday to watch The Open."

Slowly a typical Thursday Open leaderboard of unexpected guests emerged with two other players joining van Rooyen on 67. Tony Finau continued his strong showing at the first two majors of the year with a round that included eight birdies, the most anyone achieved all day. "The variety of clubs I'm hitting off the tee is pretty crazy, from driver to eight-iron," said the 28-year-old from Utah. "I've never played a course with so many options. It makes it fun." Zander Lombard, a compatriot of van Rooyen, made his score going out with four birdies. His 32 to the turn was the lowest of the round and a hiccup at the 10th was recovered with a four at the 14th.

A birdie putt fails to drop for Justin Thomas at the 18th.

Kevin Chappell exhorts a putt to slow down at the 12th.

Spain's Jon Rahm stayed aggressive on two-under-par.

Attacking from the tee, Rory McIlroy returned a 69.

Brandon Stone, who won the Aberdeen Standard Investments Scottish Open the previous week at Gullane with a final round of 60, was also flying the flag for South Africa with a 68 and even found time afterwards to nip down to St Andrews and play the Old Course with hickory clubs. Sticking to his hi-tech modern weapons, McIlroy made three birdies and only one bogey in a 69 that put him alongside Danny Willett, in a welcome return to form for the 2016 Masters champion, Rahm, PGA champion Justin Thomas and 2015 Champion Golfer Zach Johnson.

McIlroy admitted he did not see much of the fairways. The Northern Irishman felt that as long as he avoided the bunkers the course was playable even off the fairway. "If you play aggressively around here, you might make more bogeys than playing it safe but you're going to make more birdies as well," he reasoned. "You're going to give yourself more birdie looks. After the fifth hole, I didn't look like making bogey until 16 when I missed the green but got up and down. Obviously, I got

Scottish Open winner Brandon Stone signs off with a 68.

Eagles at the sixth and the 14th for Matthew Southgate.

A 69 for Danny Willett despite bunker issues at the 18th.

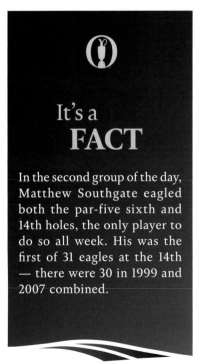

It's a
FACT

In the second group of the day, Matthew Southgate eagled both the par-five sixth and 14th holes, the only player to do so all week. His was the first of 31 eagles at the 14th — there were 30 in 1999 and 2007 combined.

Defending Champion Jordan Spieth collected the second of his three birdies at the fourth hole.

away with some tee shots, but at the same time, I think that's what I have to do."

Matt Kuchar, the runner-up at Birkdale a year earlier, started steadily with a one-under-par 70 along with 2016 Champion Golfer Henrik Stenson and Francesco Molinari. Five birdies was no surprise for the Italian given his fine results of late, but four bogeys, including at two of the last three holes, meant he was not quite as consistent as usual.

Spieth, with little recent form behind him, and Justin Rose, one of his playing partners, both scored 72. Spieth appeared to be settling into his routine from Royal Birkdale with three birdies by the 11th but then he found a bunker with his second at the 15th. His recovery squirted across the fairway into the rough and he took a double-bogey. Bogeys followed at the 16th and 18th holes as four shots went on Carnoustie's fearsome final four.

"It felt like a missed opportunity," admitted the Texan. "I felt like I was really going well. My swing just didn't quite hold up to

A visit to a bunker at the 14th prevents Francesco Molinari making a birdie.

Round of the Day: Kevin Kisner – 66

OFFICIAL SCORECARD
THE 147TH OPEN
CARNOUSTIE

Kevin KISNER ✓
Game 8
Thursday 19 July at 7.52 am

FOR R&A USE ONLY 8.2

ROUND 1
18 HOLE TOTAL

THIS ROUND 66   66
VERIFIED Q

ROUND 1

Hole	1	2	3	4	5	6	7	8	9	Out	10	11	12	13	14	15	16	17	18	In	Total
Yards	396	461	350	415	412	580	410	187	474	3685	465	382	503	175	513	472	248	460	499	3717	7402
Par	4	4	4	4	4	5	4	3	4	36	4	4	4	3	5	4	3	4	4	35	71
Score	4	4	4	4	5	3	4	2	4	34	4	4	4	2	4	3	3	4	4	32	66

Signature of Marker: _Thompson_ ✓

Signature of Competitor: Kevin Kisner

the end of my round, but it's the decision-making that's cost me. That second shot at the 15th, I just had a brain fart. I missed it into the location where the pot bunker was the only place where I could get in trouble and it plugged deep."

Rose was plodding along until his own double-bogey, a seven at the 14th. A rare three at the 18th at least salvaged something from the day. "It was an important birdie on 18, especially on a hole you can easily make bogey," he said. "It's one less birdie I need to make by Sunday. They are all important."

Perhaps the most eventful round of the day came from Koepka, who arrived after defending his US Open title at Shinnecock Hills. After a birdie at the first, he dropped six strokes in five holes from the fifth. His double-bogey there came from overshooting the green and finishing on the third tee. From there he putted back to the green while marshals held up a bunch of power cables away from his line. Another double came at the short eighth when he tried to play a bunker shot while resting on his knees outside the trap. A more conventional recovery got him out at the second attempt.

However, the American came home in 31 with five birdies and only one more bogey for another 72. "I played really well," he said. "Even that five-hole stretch I had, I felt like I played really well. Sometimes links golf just isn't the most rewarding on good shots."

Also on 72 were Fleetwood and two amateurs, Sam Locke and Denmark's Nicolai Højgaard, as well as Haraldur Magnus, the very first player from Iceland to play in The Open. "I holed a few good putts and I could definitely hear the crowd making some noise," said the 27-year-old professional from Reykjavik. "That was exciting because this is my World Cup."

And finally came Woods, teeing-off in The Open for the first

An Open best 68 for Brendan Steele.

Tiger Woods opened with a level-par 71.

Iceland's first Open competitor, Haraldur Magnus.

time since St Andrews in 2015 and late in the day alongside Russell Knox and Hideki Matsuyama. This was the venue where Woods was first introduced to links golf at the 1995 Scottish Open. Then he spent hours enthralled simply hitting as many different shots as he could conjure to the 100-yard board on the practice range.

Now he slotted straight back into the style which won him a third Claret Jug at Royal Liverpool in 2006 on similarly firm fairways. Two early birdies promised much but he could not take advantage of the par fives and ended with a 71.

"I played better than what the score indicates," Woods said. "If I just clean up those two holes, I'd have had one of the better rounds in the afternoon wave.

"I haven't played this Championship for a few years now and I've always loved playing over here. This is how the game should be played. You should be able to utilise the ground as an ally. It should be creative."

FIRST ROUND LEADERS

HOLE	1	2	3	4	5	6	7	8	9	10	11	12	13	14	15	16	17	18	TOTAL
PAR	4	4	4	4	4	5	4	3	4	4	4	4	3	5	4	3	4	4	
Kevin Kisner	4	4	4	4	5	3	4	2	4	4	4	4	2	4	3	3	4	4	66
Erik van Rooyen	3	3	4	4	4	4	4	3	4	4	3	4	3	5	3	3	4	5	67
Tony Finau	3	3	5	4	4	4	5	3	3	4	4	5	2	4	3	4	4	3	67
Zander Lombard	4	3	4	3	4	4	2	4	5	4	4	3	4	3	4	4	3	4	67
Brandon Stone	4	4	4	3	4	4	4	2	4	4	4	3	4	5	4	3	4	4	68
Ryan Moore	4	3	4	3	3	4	5	2	5	4	4	5	3	5	4	2	4	4	68
Brendan Steele	4	4	4	4	5	4	4	3	3	4	3	5	3	4	4	3	3	4	68

■ EAGLE OR BETTER   ■ BIRDIES   □ PAR   ■ OVER PAR

SCORING SUMMARY

FIRST ROUND SCORES

Players Under Par	31
Players At Par	18
Players Over Par	107

LOW SCORES

Low First Nine
Zander Lombard — 32

Low Second Nine
Brooks Koepka — 31

Low Round
Kevin Kisner — 66

FIRST ROUND HOLE SUMMARY

HOLE	PAR	YARDS	EAGLES	BIRDIES	PARS	BOGEYS	D.BOGEYS	OTHER	RANK	AVERAGE
1	4	396	0	19	113	23	0	1	14	4.045
2	4	461	0	21	91	38	6	0	T7	4.186
3	4	350	0	14	117	23	2	0	12	4.083
4	4	415	0	29	102	24	1	0	16	3.981
5	4	412	0	10	102	39	4	1	5	4.256
6	5	580	6	70	65	13	1	1	17	4.590
7	4	410	0	7	112	35	1	1	6	4.218
8	3	187	0	16	104	31	5	0	10	3.160
9	4	474	0	18	94	41	3	0	T7	4.186
OUT	36	3,685	6	204	900	267	23	4		36.705
10	4	465	0	22	99	27	7	1	11	4.141
11	4	382	0	27	95	30	4	0	13	4.071
12	4	503	0	9	82	60	4	1	2	4.397
13	3	175	0	22	109	24	1	0	15	3.026
14	5	513	0	76	59	13	2	0	18	4.545
15	4	472	0	14	103	36	3	0	9	4.179
16	3	248	0	4	85	60	5	2	1	3.462
17	4	460	0	6	101	42	7	0	3	4.321
18	4	499	0	16	94	33	8	5	4	4.314
IN	35	3,717	6	196	827	325	41	9		36.455
TOTAL	71	7,402	12	400	1,727	592	64	13		73.160

" If I have 22 putts the next three days, I bet I'll have a pretty good shot. "
—Kevin Kisner

" I think Tiger is the best player of all time and I look up to him. He is like a mythical figure. The Open in Scotland, playing with my hero. I was never going to be comfortable. It was a dream come true. "
—Russell Knox

" It's fun seeing a place as burnt out and fast as this. Some shots you are trying to hit in the air to keep it from running too much, and others you can go ahead and use the ground and let it run out. You definitely have to pick wisely. "
—Rickie Fowler

" I missed Sandy Lyle in his prime, but you can tell he's still got it — 60 years of age, he's fantastic. It was a real pleasure to watch and play with one of the greats of the game. "
—Andy Sullivan

" I told The R&A, you guys have it right, let the course get baked but you've got the greens still receptive. They're not going to be out of control. The course is set up perfect. "
—Pat Perez

" This is Scotland, five-under might win or five-over might win. "
—Jordan Spieth

" I feel like my game is built for major championship golf. "
—Tony Finau

" There's a lot to gauge. You've got to keep your head on all the time. "
—Padraig Harrington

Welcome to the House of Fun

Peter Dixon on the American players bonding as housemates in Carnoustie

Zach Johnson

Rickie Fowler

It is one of the more charming mental images from The 147th Open. It's the moment when a chastened Jordan Spieth, Champion Golfer in 2017, is to be found knocking on the door of a house in Carnoustie and asking sheepishly if he could have his football back, the one he had knocked over the fence in a kickabout with his housemates.

These were no normal housemates, however. Sharing accommodation for the week of The Open were seven of America's leading players who between them could boast eight major championships. As well as Spieth, there was Justin Thomas, Zach Johnson, Jimmy Walker, Jason Dufner, Kevin Kisner and Rickie Fowler spread across two adjoining properties.

Giving the lie to the notion that players from the other side of the Pond would rather spend time alone than bonding with their rivals, this was the third year in succession that this particular group, with the addition of Kisner at Carnoustie, had formed their own house party.

For the first gathering in 2016, Johnson arrived as the reigning Champion Golfer of the Year following his victory at St Andrews, but it was Spieth who reclaimed the Claret Jug for the house in their second year. For the first three days at Carnoustie, the formula once again seemed to be working to perfection. Kisner led the field outright after the first round and shared the lead in the second and third rounds with Johnson and Spieth respectively.

Kisner, along with Fowler, was one of only two players in the group still to win a major and yet he was completely at home in such company. In the evenings, they would sit down together for a meal prepared by the British chef they had brought over from the United States and talk through their days, sharing and gleaning information.

"Everybody will tell their horror stories and good stories and we'll laugh and eat a big old meal and sit around and watch something stupid on Netflix," Kisner revealed. "Being with them is not intimidating at all. I mean, we're out there playing soccer at night and hanging out. It's really cool just to hear what they have to say. Everybody's sitting around scratching their head on what club to hit on every tee."

Despite the camaraderie, each one of these players was in a fiercely competitive mode from the moment they arrived on the Angus links. In this instance, business still came first. Most revealing, perhaps, were the words of Thomas, the 2017 PGA champion and childhood friend of Spieth. "Obviously we want to beat each other's brains in," he said. "I never want to lose to any of my friends, especially my best friends.

"As weird as it is, it's sometimes harder losing to your close friends than it is to someone you don't even know. Then again, when I missed the cut last year, I was pulling for Jordan to win. You want to see your friend win if you can't." After missing the cut once again, Thomas was left to cheer from the sidelines, as was Walker.

After a second round of 67, Johnson found himself on six-under-par and sharing the lead with Kisner. It would be stretching a point to say that at 42 he was the old-timer in the house — Dufner came in at 41, Walker at 39 — but he admitted to feeling a little long in the tooth alongside the likes of Spieth, Thomas and Fowler, all of whom were in their 20s.

"I wasn't in a fraternity in college but it kind of feels like I'm going back to my alma mater and I'm the old guy stepping into the current frat house," he said. "It does make the week significantly easier because of the amenities we have and because I'm with buddies ... guys I can feed off and vice versa."

A family man, Kisner, 34, had a refreshing sense

Kevin Kisner

of perspective and was keen not to think too deeply about the task ahead of him or the company he was keeping. "I learned that everybody's going through the same stuff and trying to shoot the lowest score possible," he said. "Everybody puts their pants on the same way I do, probably left leg first."

By the end of the third round, however, there were small signs that things were changing. "It's the end of the week. Everybody has a lot of stuff going on. Everybody's going their separate ways tomorrow," Kisner said. For his part, Spieth jokingly suggested that he'd get the chef to try the food first, "just in case Kiz is greasing him!"

One deal remained happily in place, however. If any of them were to succeed in lifting the Claret Jug, they would pay for a private jet to fly them all back home. And what a party that would be.

A Spirited Effort from Tommy

By Andy Farrell

In two senses the natural order of things was restored for the second round of The 147th Open.

Rain returned to the east coast of Scotland in the morning, taking the fire out of the fairways and forcing players to adapt their strategies, while Carnoustie's 18th hole exerted its influence on the top of the leaderboard as few other finishing holes can.

In all a precious quarter of an inch of rain fell, heavily for a brief spell, but by the time the sun came out in the afternoon, conditions could not have been better again. Overall for the day, scoring was a third of a stroke lower than on Thursday. But the leading score moved only from five to six-under-par as the leaderboard bunched up.

'Home', the 18th hole of the Championship Course, can take the credit for that. With the hole cut on the right of the green, in a similar position to the final day of The Open in 2007, there were more birdies than in the first round (19 to 16) and, too, more double-bogeys or worse

A birdie at the 18th and a 65 for Tommy Fleetwood.

(15 to 13). There were those who walked off the green with a smile — new co-leader Zach Johnson, Tommy Fleetwood, Justin Rose and Sandy Lyle among them — and those who had to stifle a scowl, including first-round leader Kevin Kisner.

"It just helps, doesn't it?" said Fleetwood, who holed from 15 feet at the last for a birdie that briefly tied the lead and left the Lancashire golfer one behind at the end of the day. "I had a great read off Henrik Stenson. It makes such a difference to birdie the last hole with a nice putt and I did come in with a smile."

Usually distinctive for his long locks, Fleetwood was unmissable on this occasion as he spent much of his round sheltering under a yellow Open umbrella. An opening 72 had been followed by an hour's practice on the range late on Thursday evening. Whatever clicked, it was still there in the morning as Fleetwood's impeccable ball-striking produced not only the lowest score to date, a six-under-par 65, but the first and only scorecard during the first two days without a dropped shot.

Twice he pitched close for birdies at the fourth and 11th holes, while his putter was also in good form as he holed from 25 feet at the fifth, 30 feet

Round of the Day: Tommy Fleetwood – 65

OFFICIAL SCORECARD
THE 147TH OPEN
CARNOUSTIE

Tommy FLEETWOOD
Game 6
Friday 20 July at 7.30 am

	FOR R&A USE ONLY 62	ROUND 2
18 HOLE TOTAL	72	36 HOLE TOTAL
THIS ROUND	65	
36 HOLE TOTAL	137	137

VERIFIED _SmG_

ROUND 2

Hole	1	2	3	4	5	6	7	8	9	Out	10	11	12	13	14	15	16	17	18	In	Total
Yards	396	461	350	415	412	580	410	187	474	3685	465	382	503	175	513	472	248	460	499	3717	7402
Par	4	4	4	4	4	5	4	3	4	36	4	4	4	3	5	4	3	4	4	35	71
Score	4	4	4	3	3	5	4	3	3	33	4	3	4	3	4	4	3	4	4	32	65

Signature of Marker

Signature of Competitor _Tommy Fleetwood_

A 40-footer falls for Zach Johnson at the last.

at the ninth and two-putted from long range at the 14th. And then came the bonus at the last. Fleetwood was the runner-up to Brooks Koepka at the US Open after a closing 63 at Shinnecock Hills. He is no stranger to going low. He broke the Carnoustie course record with his 63 in the Alfred Dunhill Links Championship in October 2017.

Conditions nine months previously were less searching than in mid-summer and the pins for the pro-am less exacting, yet Fleetwood struggled to compare the two rounds. "It's close. It's no course record but it will do for today," he said. "Conditions-wise it was tough and you're in The Open. It was a spirited effort today."

Europe's number one from 2017 now sat as the leading British player on the leaderboard with talk inevitably turning to the prospect of a first English winner since Nick Faldo in 1992. "If I could pick one tournament in my life to win, it would be The Open," he said. "I've never been anywhere near before. So far for two rounds I'm right up there but it's about where you finish after 72 holes.

"The round at Shinnecock was very special and very close to being a one-and-only round. You can't get a tougher test than Shinnecock or Carnoustie and it's great to have the ability to shoot good scores when you're on the toughest tests in golf."

Overnight leader Kevin Kisner got to eight-under-par before a double-bogey at the last hole.

It was no surprise to see Zach Johnson scooting up the leaderboard as he added a 67 to his opening 69. It meant that he had featured in the top 20 at The Open in 23 of his last 29 rounds. Not bad for a player who missed his first three cuts before playing 72 holes for the first time at Carnoustie in 2007. The 2015 Champion Golfer of the Year actually hit his worst shot of the day off the first tee, a low three-iron pulled into the rough, for his only bogey, but then got into his stride with three birdies in four holes from the third, a four at the 14th and then a fifth birdie arrived when his 40-footer at the last dived into the hole.

"I am very happy," said the 42-year-old from Iowa. "I'm not going to say I just love playing in the wind and the rain, because I don't, but I can do it. I'm going to go out and fight. I have a great reverence for this Championship and the Claret Jug, how the game was formed over here, how The Open came into fruition in 1860, everything about it I've embraced and love."

When Johnson finished at six-under-par, Kisner, his fellow American and housemate for the week, was only just beginning his round. A theme of the day was players approaching the lead but not quite pushing forward. Rory McIlroy adapted his game plan for the conditions and ended up with a second 69 to be four-under-par. He was one stroke better after birdies at the 13th and the 14th but then dropped his second shot of the day at

Francesco Molinari suffered a double-bogey at the 17th during a 72 that left the Italian at level-par.

the 15th. "Today was a day not to shoot yourself out of the tournament," McIlroy said. "I had to tough it out at times but I kept level-headed, put my head down and got on with it."

A little further down the leaderboard, Francesco Molinari, whose 70 on Thursday might have been better without the bogeys at the 16th and 17th holes, again struggled coming in. This time he bogeyed the 15th and had a double at the 17th when he could not escape from a bunker at the first attempt. But his 72 left the Italian not so badly positioned at level-par alongside Tiger Woods, who posted a second consecutive 71. It was a scrambling effort for the former world number one from the moment he hit his tee shot

Leaderboard				Round 2			
	TOT	HOLE	RND	POS		TOT	HOLE	RND
KISNER, Kevin	-5	12.53 PM		T2 FINAU, Tony	-4	3.32 PM	
FLEETWOOD, Tommy	-4	15	-5	T2 LOMBARD, Zander	-4	3.54 PM	
MCILROY, Rory	-4	13	-2	T8 OLESEN, Thorbjorn	-3	13	-2
JOHNSON, Zach	-4	11	-2	T8 MOLINARI, Francesco	-3	11	-2
VAN ROOYEN, Erik	-4	11.47 AM		T8 DAY, Jason	-3	10	-3

A birdie at the 14th helped Rory McIlroy to another 69 and four-under-par.

"As Tommy Fleetwood charged up the leaderboard, the roars reverberated around Carnoustie. On a dreich morning on the east coast of Scotland, the Englishman's performance was just the tonic needed to lift the spirits of the drenched spectators."

—Stuart Fraser,
The Times

"Even Lyle's playing partner, Andy Sullivan — born the year after Lyle won The Open in 1985 — applauded the 60-year-old on to the final green in appreciation of one of the sport's finest ambassadors and one of Scotland's greatest sportsmen."

—Jock MacVicar,
Daily Express

"Rory McIlroy insisted he would still rather crash and burn at Carnoustie this weekend than freeze in the fear of failure."

—Neil McLeman,
Daily Mirror

"Although Woods appeared relatively content, surely there was some angst over a missed birdie putt at the last hole or the two early bogeys that put him in catch-up mode for most of a rainy day at The Open."

—Bob Harig,
ESPN

Marc Leishman plays from a ditch at the 12th hole.

A 67 and a 10-shot improvement for Masahiro Kawamura.

at the second into thick and by now wet rough. His next shot forked off towards the gallery, but fortunately the only damage was to an umbrella and the bogey on Tiger's card.

As for the overnight leader, Kisner got to seven-under-par thanks to birdies at the fifth and seventh holes. He went bogey-birdie-bogey over the next three holes, but a two at the 13th from 18 feet and a four at the 14th after getting up and down from a bunker put him to eight-under-par. Could he survive the gruelling run in? He parred the next three holes but his drive at the last found rough and his attempt to make the green with an eight-iron came up short in the burn.

Tiger Woods tees off at the 15th during his 71.

A 68 put Pat Perez one stroke off the lead.

"The way it was sitting, I didn't think it was an issue to get it in one of the bunkers by the green and have a good chance at a four," he explained. "It just came out like a high flop shot to the right. It was weird." A double-bogey-six followed, so a 70 left him tied for the lead with Johnson. "To play 35 holes without a double, I thought was pretty good. I've kept the ball in play and done everything I wanted to do up until that hole. But I hit a lot of great putts and I love my position going into the weekend."

Suddenly, the day had a different complexion with no solo leader out in front. Everyone seemed to be in contention.

Pat Perez tied for the lead when he collected his fourth birdie of the day at the 14th. He almost matched Fleetwood's feat of going bogey-free before he drove into a bunker at the last and took a five. A 68 left the 42-year-old American alongside the Englishman on five-under-par.

Adam Scott and his caddie Fanny Sunesson

John Murray of BBC Radio Five Live commentating with former Women's British Open Champion Karen Stupples.

Fanny returns for one week only

Fanny Sunesson only intended to caddie for a few months to see the world — yet in a 25-year career helped Nick Faldo to two of his three Open titles.

Having retired from her bag carrying duties, Sunesson now works as a performance coach, television commentator and helps organise a junior tournament in Sweden with another of her former bosses, Henrik Stenson. But when Adam Scott needed a caddie for The Open at Carnoustie, the former Masters champion persuaded Sunesson out of retirement — for one week only.

"It's been going great," said Scott, who was nicely placed at one-under-par at the halfway stage. "Fanny is obviously a fantastic caddie and to be able to have that experience out there with me is certainly comforting. We're getting along really well. She's picked up on my game quickly and we think about things in a very similar way. I'd like to be able to put her to the test a bit over the weekend, if we can get in contention."

Scott, who eventually finished 17th, added: "I don't think she's making plans of a comeback. I was being a bit opportunistic in contacting her and coaxing her out of retirement."

Sunesson wrote on social media: "I am grateful that Adam asked me to caddie at The Open. I loved the week! I had not caddied for almost seven years and it was fantastic to caddie again. Thank you to everyone for all your support."

Xander Schauffele, in his second Open, came home in 31 for a 66 to tie for third place.

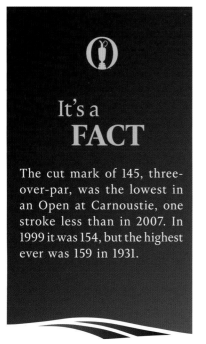

Joining them on that mark was Xander Schauffele after the best inward half of the day. Enjoying the late evening conditions, the 2017 PGA TOUR Rookie of the Year birdied the 11th, eagled the 14th and then hit his approach at the 17th to three feet to come home in 31 for a 66 that propelled him into a tie for third place.

Tony Finau had a back spasm while he was working out before his round but still managed briefly to tie for the lead. In fact, his eagle putt to get to seven-under-par at the 14th lipped out. He then bogeyed the 15th and 18th holes to finish with a 71 at four-under-par. "I could barely bend over when it happened," Finau said of the injury. "I didn't know how well I was going to be able to play or if I was going to be able to play. So I'm extremely pleased in the circumstances."

Another late challenger was Zander Lombard, a former finalist at The Amateur Championship. The 23-year-old from Pretoria birdied the third and seventh holes to get to six-under-par, dropped one and picked it up again early on the back nine but then suffered two late

A rough spot for Sergio Garcia.

Two 70s for Thorbjørn Olesen.

A smooth putting stroke for Tony Finau, who remained at four-under-par.

"Stonehaven teenager Sam Locke can look forward to the greatest weekend of his life as he spends two days strolling around the Carnoustie links with men he dreams of joining as a professional golfer, knowing he has already done enough to secure one of his sport's most coveted prizes."

—Kevin Ferrie,
The Herald

"He flies under the radar with the profile of a stealth jet. He turns self-deprecation into an art form. Conservative and boring, that's how Zach Johnson describes himself."

—John Greechan,
Daily Mail

"It was, without doubt, the biggest roar of the day. When Sandy Lyle's 25-foot birdie putt rolled into the hole, the place exploded in the sort of uproar generated when 300 cold, soggy and largely superannuated Scots salute one of their own."

—Richard Bath,
The Daily Telegraph

"On the strength of three birdies over Carnoustie's difficult closing stretch, capped by a 30-foot surprise at the punishing 18th, Kuchar rose into contention."

—Dave Shedloski,
Golf Digest

Jordan Spieth chips in for a birdie on the third hole on the way to a 67.

A 68 put Matt Kuchar two off the lead.

bogeys at the 16th and 17th holes. Like Finau, a 71 left him on four-under-par alongside compatriot Erik van Rooyen, McIlroy and Matt Kuchar. The American, who had the Claret Jug snatched away by Jordan Spieth's dramatics a year earlier, birdied three of the last six holes, including the last, to notify his intention to go one better in 2018.

Speaking of Spieth, the defending Champion got himself to three-under-par alongside countrymen Rickie Fowler and Kevin Chappell with a 67. He chipped in from behind the third green, an exquisite shot but a birdie that summed up his day. He visited far too much uncharted territory. His approach shot from the rough at the 10th, curling round the trees to set up another birdie, was another example of his recovery skills. Somehow he ended up with only one bogey on his card, that came at the 16th.

Erik van Rooyen stayed at four-under-par.

Spieth's playing partner, Rose, managed only one birdie all day but it came when most needed — at the 18th. In fact, the former US Open champion had holed a vital par-save at the 15th hole but the 15-footer he sank at the last got him back to three-over-par and right on the cut line. Despite his frustrations, he would still be around for the weekend. "The whole day the crowd are trying to cheer you up," he said, "and that almost adds to the frustration because you sense they want it for you but nothing's happening."

Rickie Fowler was three back after a 69.

Sam locks up the Silver Medal

When 19-year-old Sam Locke teed-off in the first group at 6.35am on Friday, he was one of four amateurs hoping to make the halfway cut. He had opened his account with a creditable 72 and went on to add a 73 for a three-over-par total of 145. And then his wait began...

One of the most coveted prizes at The Open is the Silver Medal, awarded to the leading amateur after the completion of four rounds. Locke, from Stonehaven, near Aberdeen, knew he was in with a chance of making the cut but would not know for certain until play finished around 9pm, 10 hours after he had walked off the 18th green.

With his rivals falling away, the 2017 Scottish Amateur champion and medallist in Final Qualifying at The Renaissance Club was subsequently delighted to find that not only had he got in on the cut line but that he was the last of the amateurs still standing.

Mentored by 1999 Champion Golfer Paul Lawrie, Locke had dropped three strokes in his first three holes but fought back with three birdies in succession from the 13th. "I just kept plugging away," he said. "You never know what's around the corner in this game. I felt that if I could keep it in play off the tee and give myself

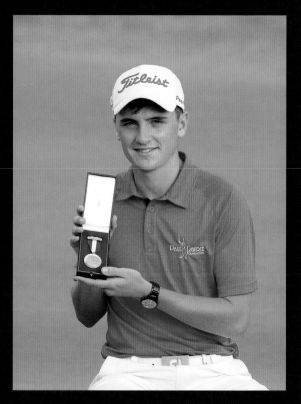

chances for birdies, a few of them are going to go in."

With further scores of 70 and 78, he finished on nine-over-par and in a share of 75th place.

Japan's Yusaku Miyazato also survived on 145 despite a triple-bogey at the last, but his compatriot Hideki Matsuyama missed out by one after his own seven at the 18th. World number two Justin Thomas's birdie putt at the last lipped out, otherwise he would have qualified, while Dustin Johnson, the world number one, was beyond saving after another disaster at 'Home'. He followed his triple-bogey on Thursday with a double on Friday. It was the first time the top two players in the world had missed the cut at The Open since Luke Donald and Lee Westwood in 2011.

Sam Locke spent all day wondering if his 145 total would be good enough to qualify for the weekend. It turned out it was and even better it won him the Silver Medal as well when none of the other amateurs made the cut.

Of the 60-year-olds, Bernhard Langer made it but Sandy Lyle did not. Nevertheless, the 1985 Champion Golfer enjoyed a bravura farewell when his birdie putt at the last found the hole. There was not a dry eye in the house and certainly not Sandy's. The 18th at Carnoustie had worked its magic once more.

A triple-bogey-seven at the last hole meant Japan's Hideki Matsuyama missed the cut.

Spieth congratulates Justin Rose on making the cut.

At 60, Bernhard Langer qualified for the weekend.

SECOND ROUND LEADERS

HOLE	1	2	3	4	5	6	7	8	9	10	11	12	13	14	15	16	17	18	TOTAL
PAR	4	4	4	4	4	5	4	3	4	4	4	4	3	5	4	3	4	4	
Zach Johnson	5	4	3	3	4	4	4	3	4	4	4	4	3	4	4	3	4	3	67-136
Kevin Kisner	4	4	4	4	3	5	3	4	3	5	4	2	4	4	4	3	4	6	70-136
Tommy Fleetwood	4	4	4	3	3	5	4	3	3	4	3	4	3	4	4	4	4	3	65-137
Pat Perez	4	4	3	4	4	5	4	3	4	4	4	4	3	4	4	3	4	5	68-137
Xander Schauffele	4	4	4	4	4	4	2	5	4	3	4	4	3	3	4	3	4	4	66-137
Rory McIlroy	4	4	4	4	5	3	4	3	4	3	4	5	2	4	5	4	4	4	69-138
Erik van Rooyen	4	5	3	4	4	5	3	3	5	5	3	4	3	5	4	3	4	4	71-138
Matt Kuchar	4	4	4	4	4	4	5	3	4	4	4	4	2	4	4	3	4	3	68-138
Tony Finau	4	3	4	4	4	5	4	3	4	5	4	3	3	4	5	3	4	5	71-138
Zander Lombard	4	4	3	4	4	5	3	3	4	4	4	5	3	4	4	4	5	4	71-138

■ EAGLE OR BETTER ■ BIRDIES ☐ PAR ■ OVER PAR

SCORING SUMMARY

SECOND ROUND SCORES

Players Under Par	38
Players At Par	25
Players Over Par	92

LOW SCORES

Low First Nine

Tommy Fleetwood	33
Masahiro Kawamura	33
Tom Lewis	33
Kyle Stanley	33

Low Second Nine

Xander Schauffele	31

Low Round

Tommy Fleetwood	65

SECOND ROUND HOLE SUMMARY

HOLE	PAR	YARDS	EAGLES	BIRDIES	PARS	BOGEYS	D.BOGEYS	OTHER	RANK	AVERAGE
1	4	396	0	12	117	23	3	0	12	4.110
2	4	461	0	16	89	45	5	0	5	4.252
3	4	350	0	34	112	8	1	0	17	3.845
4	4	415	0	24	114	16	1	0	14	3.961
5	4	412	0	23	113	17	1	1	13	3.994
6	5	580	0	27	89	26	12	1	9	5.174
7	4	410	0	18	106	23	5	3	10	4.161
8	3	187	0	13	107	33	2	0	11	3.155
9	4	474	0	16	98	35	5	1	8	4.206
OUT	36	3,685	0	183	945	226	35	6		36.858
10	4	465	0	16	93	41	5	0	T6	4.226
11	4	382	0	38	101	15	1	0	16	3.865
12	4	503	0	4	82	58	10	1	1	4.497
13	3	175	0	30	102	23	0	0	15	2.955
14	5	513	11	92	47	4	1	0	18	4.303
15	4	472	0	7	109	36	3	0	T6	4.226
16	3	248	0	11	94	43	7	0	3	3.297
17	4	460	0	8	100	44	3	0	4	4.271
18	4	499	0	19	88	33	11	4	2	4.310
IN	35	3,717	11	225	816	297	41	5		35.948
TOTAL	71	7,402	11	408	1,761	523	76	11		72.806

" I was on cloud nine walking down the 18th. It's quite a spectacular view to come down there and to make birdie was extra special. I managed to stay away from crying but definitely a lump in the throat. "

—Sandy Lyle

" I've been called 'Dustin' many times. I doubt he's been called 'Zach' that many times. "

—Zach Johnson

" We were given an official Open umbrella for free, we didn't steal it. It looked quite nice, the yellow and the course. "

—Tommy Fleetwood

" It's an amazing experience being in the thick of things. I've been in and out of leads in my career in big events — not in majors yet, but it's just a tournament with bigger stands. "

—Zander Lombard

" It didn't stop raining the whole time. It was tough because, by the end of everything, it was wet. My whole bag is wet. The clubs are wet. "

—Jason Day

" I always love a Claret Jug in my hands. Only have the replica now at my place, the original again would be nice. "

—Louis Oosthuizen

" I know I didn't play my best, but I've beaten a lot of very good players who are a lot younger than me. "

—Bernhard Langer

Learn to Adapt or Go Home Early

Alistair Tait says those players able to change their strategy were rewarded

Attacking Jon Rahm found bunker issues.

Rory McIlroy arrived for The 147th Open with a game plan: to be aggressive. However, the 2014 Champion Golfer of the Year has played enough links golf to know great championship courses like Carnoustie reward those who can adapt. Those who don't, go home early.

McIlroy did and booked his ticket for the weekend. Other notables didn't and probably left Carnoustie questioning the strategy they brought to the game's oldest major.

The 29-year-old Northern Irishman hit driver as often as possible in round one. He changed tack in round two. He had to. Morning rain changed Carnoustie's playing conditions subtly enough to oblige the former world number one to use guile, rather than force, to fashion a score around arguably the toughest course on The Open rota.

If only world number five Jon Rahm had done the same, he might have been around for the weekend too. Same with the world's top two players, Dustin Johnson and Justin Thomas.

McIlroy hit six drivers in the second round. Yet he shot the same score as day one, another 69 to make him four-under-par heading into the weekend.

"It was just damp enough and cold enough that the game plan that I was trying to adopt to be aggressive and hit driver a lot, I just couldn't do it," McIlroy said. "All the bunkers were in play. So a lot more irons off tees and a lot more conservative."

Rahm stuck to his guns, pulling driver every chance he got. He didn't factor in that the early morning rain changed the conditions such that bunkers he could carry in round one suddenly came into play.

After an opening 69, the Spaniard arrived for his afternoon tee-time with high expectations. He justified that hope by playing the first three holes in one-under-par. His decision to stick with driver cost him at the seventh when he drove out of bounds en route to a triple-bogey. A bogey at the par-three eighth ensued when his ball plugged in the greenside bunker.

His game plan came unstuck again at the ninth when he hit driver off the tee and found a horrible lie in a fairway bunker. The ensuing double-bogey meant he'd covered the last three holes of the front nine in six-over-par. He limped home with a 78.

The Spaniard refused to blame aggressive tactics for his poor round.

"I was going to make bad swings whether I had an iron or I had a driver in my hands," he said. "I have no regrets on the strategy."

He might think otherwise on reflection. He only hit seven of 15 fairways each day. He might have made the weekend if he'd taken a cannier approach.

Phil Mickelson made the cut with a 69 after a 73 in round one. He recognised Carnoustie's subtle difference and tried to go with the flow.

"It changed throughout the day entirely, and it changes the way you are trying to attack the course or play conservative," the 2013 Champion said.

World number one Johnson recognised the key to taming Carnoustie before the Championship began.

"Navigating the bunkers is definitely the biggest

ustin Thomas failed to figure out links golf.

key this week," he said. "I'm going to hit driver. If can carry all the bunkers and keep it out of them, I'm going to hit a driver."

Johnson managed to better Rahm in fairways hit, but only just. He managed 15 of 30 fairways to post scores of 76 and 72 to miss the weekend.

World number two Thomas looked like contending at Carnoustie after an opening 69. A 77 on day two put paid to that notion. He missed the cut by a shot. Thomas later tweeted: "Gonna figure out this tournament one of these years! Absolutely love @TheOpen @Carnoustie Golf Links and links golf, just have to eliminate the mistakes. Onward and upward."

Tiger Woods hit 22 fairways over the first two days to make the cut with scores of 71 and 71. After a late afternoon tee-time on day one, he turned up to find Carnoustie less fiery on Friday. Unsurprisingly, the 4-time major winner had no trouble adapting.

"It was nice that it slowed the golf course down," Woods said about the early morning rain. "We certainly had a chance to get the ball down a little bit further and control it on the ground a little bit better. The ball wasn't rolling 80, 90 yards like it was yesterday. It was a little bit easier in that regard."

As a three-time Open winner, Woods was speaking from experience. McIlroy, another holder of the Claret Jug, also had the nous to adapt. As Thomas acknowledged via social media, that's something he

Rory McIlroy had the nous to adapt his day one strategy.

Spieth Drives Back to the Top

By Andy Farrell

With one giant blow Jordan Spieth signalled the start of what would become a most thrilling weekend at The 147th Open.

Spieth and Carnoustie appeared made for each other — a player who makes things happen on a course full of drama. When Spieth, who by and large had been cautious off the tee over the first two days, pulled the driver out of his bag on the first tee on Saturday, it was time to take notice.

His drive pitched in the centre of the fairway and then, with the ground firming up again since the previous day's rain had departed, ran and ran and ran all the way on to the front of the green. With the set-up used for the third round, the hole was measuring 380 yards from tee markers to flagstick.

Spieth was only 12 feet short of the hole and, with a sense of occasion befitting a three-time major champion, duly made the eagle putt. Suddenly, his defence of the Claret Jug had gone up several notches and so had this Championship.

Spieth's fast start set Carnoustie alight on Saturday.

Apart from getting a severe short-back-and-sides from a local barber that morning, Spieth had been watching the morning scores which included a 64 from Justin Rose to tie the best score in The Open at Carnoustie. "The course seemed very gettable," Spieth said. "We were talking about hitting driver on the first while we were on the range and then when we got on the tee and the wind wasn't really blowing, I thought it was driver for sure. It was a bonus for it to get to the green and for the putt to curl in, it was a dream start to the day."

It was a day that took Spieth all the way to the top of the leaderboard with a third round of 65. At nine-under-par he was joined by Xander Schauffele and Kevin Kisner who had not been topped all week. The trio of Americans led by two from a fourth, Kevin Chappell, with Francesco Molinari a further stroke back. The Italian matched Spieth's 65 to finish one ahead of the pack at five-under-par that included a charging Tiger Woods whose 66 added even more electricity to proceedings along with a hint of nostalgia.

When Rose finished his round he was two off the lead but ended up five behind on four-under-par. Chris Wood went out in five-under-par 31 to

Rose's impeccable timing

When Justin Rose stood over a 15-foot putt for birdie at the 18th hole in the second round, he knew that he would miss the halfway cut if he failed to make it. It was 20 years to the day since he had turned professional and he was determined not to mark the occasion by bailing out of The Open early.

Needless to say, the 37-year-old Englishman was equal to the task. After pulling himself back from the brink, Rose was determined to do himself justice over the weekend. He was nine strokes off the lead heading into the third round but what unfolded over the next four hours brought the 2013 US Open champion right back into the mix, just five behind.

Justin Rose and his wife Kate

With little wind and some friendlier hole locations, Rose felt a good score was there for the asking. A birdie at the first hole was followed by another at the sixth and five more on a stunning inward half of 30. Rose's bogey-free 64 equalled the lowest score in an Open at Carnoustie set by Steve Stricker and Richard Green in 2007.

This was arguably Rose's best performance in The Open since he finished tied-fourth as a 17-year-old amateur at Royal Birkdale in 1998 and, like the Pied Piper, he started to gather the crowds around him. "It was lovely to get the crowd going," he said. "I hadn't had a lot of momentum from the crowd all week and today it started to change."

Round of the Day: Justin Rose – 64

OFFICIAL SCORECARD
THE 147TH OPEN
CARNOUSTIE

Justin ROSE ✓✓
Game 3
Saturday 21 July at 9.35 am

FOR R&A USE ONLY 22		ROUND 3
36 HOLE TOTAL 145		54 HOLE TOTAL
THIS ROUND 64		
54 HOLE TOTAL 209		209
VERIFIED JGD		

ROUND 3

Hole	1	2	3	4	5	6	7	8	9	Out
Yards	396	461	350	415	412	580	410	187	474	3685
Par	4	4	4	4	4	5	4	3	4	36
Score	3	4	4	4	4	4	4	3	4	34

Hole	10	11	12	13	14	15	16	17	18	In	Total
Yards	465	382	503	175	513	472	248	460	499	3717	7402
Par	4	4	4	3	5	4	3	4	4	35	71
Score	3	4	4	2	4	4	3	3	3	30	64

Signature of Marker

Signature of Competitor — Justin Rose

show the early starters what was possible but it was Rose who came home in a best-of-the-week 30 with five birdies, including at the 18th for the third day running. After having made a three at the 18th on Friday evening to make the cut on the mark, now he had given himself a chance of being in contention on Sunday. That's how congested the scoring was.

"It was a beautiful morning to play golf and I felt like it was an opportunity to score well out there," Rose said. "The greens were somewhat receptive and the pins weren't as tough as maybe the first couple of days. It was a typical set-up for moving day. So it was nice to make that move."

He might have hoped for the breeze to pick up in the afternoon and evening but, in fact, conditions remained favourable all day. For the first time in any round of The Open at Carnoustie, the scoring average of 70.23 was under par.

A 65 for Japan's Yusaku Miyazato.

Woods was determined not to miss out. His strategy changed as he took the driver out on at least half a dozen occasions but it worked in the sense that no one for the first three rounds had better fairways-hit statistics than Tiger. It also worked on the scorecard.

After birdies at the fourth and sixth holes, it was the hat-trick of threes from the ninth that got another huge gallery excited. At the 14th he had an eagle putt to take the lead on his own. It just missed but at six-under-par he was briefly tied for the lead. He dropped a shot at the 16th but saved par at the last after a wayward drive almost finished in the Barry Burn.

His 66 was his lowest score in The Open since a 65 in the second round at Royal Liverpool in 2006 when he won for the third time. But the mistakes at the end, 10 years on from his last major

Chris Wood posted an early 66.

Holding nothing back, Francesco Molinari moved into contention with a six-under-par 65.

victory and four back surgeries later, hinted the 42-year-old might not quite be back on winning form.

Not so for Molinari. The 35-year-old from Turin arrived in the form of his life. He won the BMW PGA Championship at Wentworth, was second in the Italian Open, 25th in the US Open, then won Tiger's own tournament, the Quicken Loans National, and was second at the John Deere Classic. Over the first two days he had collected plenty of birdies, nine in all, but had been held back by seven bogeys and a double-bogey.

Nothing held him back on Saturday. He birdied the first, the sixth and the seventh to turn in 33, then added a three at the 10th, a four at the 14th and, one of the highlights of the day, holed a putt from off the right side of the 16th green for a two. For weeks, it seemed, if not months and years, Molinari's long game had been robotically repetitive. Drives heading straight down the fairway, approach shots zeroing in on the flagstick. At the 18th now, he gave himself another chance from five feet and just pulled it wide.

Tiger Woods plays his second at the 18th after just missing the burn.

Kevin Chappell started with three birdies in a row and claimed the only three of the day at the 12th hole.

Rickie Fowler found trouble at the sixth and took an eight.

Once this would have been an example of the Italian's chronic weakness, not holing enough short putts, but after the work he has done with putting coach Phil Kenyon, it was more of a surprise. "I played well and had quite a few chances that went close by, so it could have been even better," he admitted. "It was the day to be aggressive and I'm really happy where I am at the moment. Tomorrow might be a different story but if I do the things I did well today, go through my process all the time for 18 holes, any conditions are the same."

By now Spieth was charging ahead. After the eagle at the first, he birdied the fourth where his ball obeyed instructions long after he had hit his approach. "One big hop, now whoa there," he commanded and the ball stopped on the second bounce two feet from the hole. At the 11th he hit a drive and a wedge to five feet then he two-putted

Spieth acknowledges the gallery after his eagle at the first hole.

EXCERPTS FROM THE PRESS

"If Carnoustie made Saturdays... This was as good as it gets, as captivating as any 11-hour golfing day could ever wish to be."
—James Corrigan,
The Sunday Telegraph

"McIlroy's driving was magnificent and mostly straight. The recurring problem was distance control with his short irons. He should have been peppering the pins but he wasn't."
—Denis Walsh,
The Sunday Times

"Jordan Spieth wandered into a Carnoustie barbers for a dodgy trim before cutting through the field to head the leaderboard at The Open."
—Euan McLean,
Sunday Mail

"If the German football team played like Bernhard Langer did yesterday, they would have walked away with the World Cup in Russia this summer."
—Tony Stenson,
Daily Star Sunday

"Tiger Woods sprinkled the magic beans on a day to remember at The Open, but it was Jordan Spieth who climbed the beanstalk to hit the front in his bid for back-to-back Claret Jugs."
—Neil Squires,
Sunday Express

for a four at the 14th to get to eight-under-par. He had struggled on the closing stretch for the first two days but not now. At the 16th, where he had two bogeys to his name, he hit a five-iron to 10 feet and made a two.

Other than a fine up-and-down at the 12th, he had not been in much trouble. A year earlier he had been leading by three with a round to play but still needed a once-in-a-lifetime finish to lift the Claret Jug. "I felt I had something to prove last year, really to myself more than anything," Spieth admitted.

"I don't feel I've got anything to prove to anyone at this point. I'm playing golf for myself. It's been a bit of an off year but I've been making progress with my game and I've got an opportunity to make it a memorable one tomorrow. But I'm not getting ahead of myself. After the first round I just wanted to give myself a chance and I've done well the last two days."

A reminder that Carnoustie could still sting came when Rickie Fowler made an eight at the sixth hole after going out of bounds. A 73 took him out of the reckoning. Playing alongside Spieth,

South Africa's Zander Lombard celebrates after making an eagle-two at the 18th hole.

A level-par 71 for Erik van Rooyen.

Webb Simpson scored a 67 with a little help from caddie Paul Tesori.

A study in contrasts on the 18th green: a bogey and a 67 for Alex Noren (left), a par and a 70 for Matt Kuchar.

Chappell birdied the first three holes, claimed the only three of the day at the 12th, and went on to return a 67.

But quite a few of the leading players could not get going to the same degree. There were 71s for Tony Finau and the South Africans Erik van Rooyen and Zander Lombard, although Lombard made a dramatic finish by following a double-bogey at the 17th with an eagle at the last by holing his wedge from 132 yards. They remained at four-under-par, while Matt Kuchar got to five-under with a 70. He joined Woods on that mark, as well as Alex Noren and Webb Simpson, who both scored 67s. Also ending up on five-under were Rory McIlroy after a 70, Tommy Fleetwood with a 71, and Zach Johnson after a 72.

It was a "rocky" ride for Tommy Fleetwood as the Englishman slipped down the leaderboard with a 71.

Byeong Hun An completes a 66 with a par at the last.

A happy 22nd birthday for India's Shubhankar Sharma.

After his low round on Friday, Fleetwood went out near the top of The Open leaderboard on the weekend for the first time, and although he was steady through the front nine, coming home he had four birdies, two pars, two bogeys and a double. "It was a bit rocky coming home," he said. "I actually felt more comfortable with my swing than yesterday. It just shows what can go into scoring in this silly game."

McIlroy also failed to take advantage despite getting to three-under-par for his round and seven-under-par for the Championship after 15 holes. Dropped shots at the 16th and 18th holes left him four behind instead of within two of the lead. "The course was perfectly set up to attack and I've tried to do that," said the 2014 Champion Golfer of the Year. "Maybe my wedge play was not quite as good as it should have been but I gave myself plenty of chances. I just need to get off to a good start tomorrow."

Of his twoball, McIlroy might have been expected to be the main challenger but Schauffele, in only his second Open, produced a 67 to tie Spieth. The

Another fine driving display from Rory McIlroy, but two late dropped shots left him four strokes off the lead.

Like the old days for Langer

Aged 60 and still dominant on the Champions Tour, Bernhard Langer performed a Saturday morning links masterclass. Having made the cut in his 31st Open appearance, the German enjoyed a 23rd round in the 60s with a 68 that included an eagle at the 14th and a birdie at the 17th. "It was a good day in the office," he said. "Hit some great iron shots and played a lot better."

A large gallery was thrilled by the exhibition. "It was almost like the old days," Langer said. "People really appreciate what I've done in my career and that I'm still here at age 60 and still playing decent golf."

In his long career in The Open dating back to 1976, Langer was never a Champion Golfer of the Year despite six top-three finishes. "It's been a good run," he reflected. "I came close. It's the one I wanted and I didn't get. What can you do? I've been blessed with two Masters titles and many other victories. Still, good to be back."

Langer qualified by winning The Senior Open presented by Rolex for a third time at Royal Porthcawl in 2017. As he holed out at the 18th at Carnoustie on Sunday, Langer admitted thinking this may be his last appearance in The Open — unless he could win a record fourth Senior Open the following week at St Andrews. He nearly did, too, losing by just one stroke to Miguel Ángel Jiménez.

EXCERPTS
FROM THE PRESS

"The last three Opens at Carnoustie have all required play-offs to determine the Champion Golfer of the Year. Another four-hole shoot-out for the Claret Jug could be in the offing at the Angus venue as it's tight at the top heading into the final circuit in the 147th staging of golf's oldest major."

—Martin Dempster,
Scotland on Sunday

"When Tiger Woods batted away questions about his aching neck, he was speaking the language of the new Supermen, the elite veterans of sport who rebuild their bodies and forge on towards middle age, reluctant or unable to walk away from the calling that defines them. If you wanted to believe a man can fly, Tiger came close to proving it here."

—Kevin Mitchell,
The Observer

"Woods had largely been eschewing his driver in the previous two days to avoid Carnoustie's daunting rough, but on Saturday, he had no compunction about pulling out the longest club in the bag."

—Bill Pennington,
The New York Times

Xander Schauffele celebrates his birdie at the 18th to tie for the lead.

Overnight leader Zach Johnson drives at the 12th hole, where a double-bogey halted his challenge.

24-year-old from San Diego finished 20th at Royal Birkdale on his debut and had a simple attitude to golf at the British seaside. "Try to have some fun, stay out of the pot bunkers and make some putts," he said.

His "SoCal vibe", Schauffele figured, helped him cope with playing alongside McIlroy. "I played in front of what you might call Rory's crowd and guys were yelling all the time, even when he was putting. He had to step off a few times but no one was yelling at me while I was putting. It didn't bother me at all."

Winning the Tour Championship in the US to cap his rookie season may have raised expectations and although Schauffele had not added to his two wins from 2017, his best two results so far were second at THE PLAYERS Championship and sixth at the US Open. "It might just be coincidence but hopefully not," he said. "I have more fun at the big events."

A 67 for American Austin Cook on his Open debut.

A steady bogey-free round of 68 kept Kevin Kisner in a three-way share of the lead after three rounds.

Schauffele was having fun now, overcoming an early bogey with three birdies in a row from the fifth. He then birdied three of the last five, bouncing back from a five at the 17th to make a three at the last. At two-under-par for the last four holes for three days, only Rose at four-under-par had played the closing stretch better than Schauffele so far.

With so much going on elsewhere, attention only fleetingly returned to the overnight leaders, as when Johnson holed a monster putt at the sixth for an eagle. But it was an inconsistent day for the former Champion and he tangled with a bush for a double-bogey at the 12th as he fell four strokes off the lead.

Kisner, however, was wonderfully steady as he matched his feat from the 2017 PGA Championship of leading for the first three days. He hit close at the third for the first of three birdies, the

others coming at the two par fives. "I didn't hole the amount of putts I had the first two days, but conditions got tough coming down the stretch and I made a couple of nice par putts coming in," he said of his bogey-free 68. "I put myself in a perfect position to have a chance to win. I was hitting it really solid and that is going to be a huge help tomorrow with the wind blowing."

That was the forecast, for players to face the strongest wind yet on Sunday, but forecasting the result was almost impossible. Was Spieth now the man with it to lose, or was it still a wide-open Open? Spieth said: "I've always wanted to battle it out in a major with Tiger. Who hasn't? It's a dream come true to have that opportunity."

Careful what you wish for, was the immediate reaction. Hindsight revealed that this would be far more than a two-man contest. More like six or seven. What a day in prospect.

THIRD ROUND LEADERS

HOLE	1	2	3	4	5	6	7	8	9	10	11	12	13	14	15	16	17	18	TOTAL
PAR	4	4	4	4	4	5	4	3	4	4	4	4	3	5	4	3	4	4	TOTAL
Jordan Spieth	2	4	4	3	4	5	4	3	4	4	3	4	3	4	4	2	4	4	65-204
Xander Schauffele	4	5	4	4	3	4	3	3	4	4	4	4	3	3	3	5	3		67-204
Kevin Kisner	4	4	3	4	4	4	3	4	4	4	4	3	4	4	3	4	4		68-204
Kevin Chappell	3	3	3	4	4	6	4	3	5	4	4	3	4	4	3	4	3		67-206
Francesco Molinari	3	4	4	4	4	4	3	3	4	3	4	4	3	4	4	2	4	4	65-207

■ EAGLE OR BETTER ■ BIRDIES □ PAR ■ OVER PAR

SCORING SUMMARY

THIRD ROUND SCORES

Players Under Par	41
Players At Par	14
Players Over Par	24

LOW SCORES

Low First Nine	
Chris Wood	31
Low Second Nine	
Justin Rose	30
Low Round	
Justin Rose	64

THIRD ROUND HOLE SUMMARY

HOLE	PAR	YARDS	EAGLES	BIRDIES	PARS	BOGEYS	D.BOGEYS	OTHER	RANK	AVERAGE
1	4	396	1	15	57	5	1	0	14	3.873
2	4	461	0	16	52	11	0	0	T10	3.937
3	4	350	0	11	51	16	1	0	6	4.089
4	4	415	0	21	49	8	1	0	15	3.861
5	4	412	0	16	54	9	0	0	12	3.911
6	5	580	1	33	34	8	2	1	17	4.747
7	4	410	0	15	59	4	1	0	13	3.886
8	3	187	0	9	59	11	0	0	7	3.025
9	4	474	0	9	50	20	0	0	4	4.139
OUT	**36**	**3,685**	**2**	**145**	**465**	**92**	**6**	**1**		**35.468**
10	4	465	0	14	56	7	2	0	T8	3.962
11	4	382	0	23	48	8	0	0	16	3.810
12	4	503	0	1	45	25	8	0	1	4.506
13	3	175	0	12	60	7	0	0	T10	2.937
14	5	513	11	53	11	4	0	0	18	4.101
15	4	472	0	13	57	8	1	0	T8	3.962
16	3	248	0	5	53	20	1	0	2	3.215
17	4	460	0	9	50	18	2	0	3	4.165
18	4	499	1	13	45	17	3	0	5	4.101
IN	**35**	**3,717**	**12**	**143**	**425**	**114**	**17**	**0**		**34.759**
TOTAL	**71**	**7,402**	**14**	**288**	**890**	**206**	**23**	**1**		**70.228**

66 This is the best birthday gift for me, just playing in The Open. Perfect. Perfect weather. It's the best way to spend my birthday. 99
—Shubhankar Sharma

66 The way I've played the first couple of days has been terrible, so to shoot in the mid-60s today, regardless of how I finished, was a good effort. 99
—Chris Wood

66 I have never played with Tiger before. It's absolutely crazy to think so many people can follow a person. A couple of holes people were standing 15, 20 deep on each side. 99
—Shaun Norris

66 I said to my caddie walking down the fairway, 'let's have a good finish for the crowds at least.' A two on the 18th at The Open on Saturday was good. 99
—Zander Lombard

66 The game's just hard for me right now. I don't feel I'm playing bad, it's just not coming easy. 99
—Phil Mickelson

66 The crowds were unbelievable. I know they were greeting Jordan, The Open Champion from last year, but you still can't help but get goosebumps yourself. 99
—Kevin Chappell

66 That's my fondest memory of The Open so far, walking up 18 and feeling it from all the people. I love the energy. It's incredible, honestly. 99
—Tony Finau

Tiger a Leader Once Again

Art Spander sees a familiar name back at the top of the leaderboard

Everything had changed. Nothing had changed. That name up there above the others on the leaderboards, so familiar, so strange. Tiger Woods? Where did he come from? Out of the pack? Out of our memories? Out of a dream?

It was St Andrews 2000 and 2005, Royal Liverpool 2006. It was Carnoustie 2018 and the crowds were hooting and hollering — "Go get 'em, Tiger" — as they did years earlier when Eldrick Woods, now 42, virtually owned golf.

Woods leading The Open; after heaven knows how many back surgeries and months of rehabilitation; after finishing 32nd in the Masters; after missing the cut in the US Open at Shinnecock Hills. Impossible. Wonderful.

Tiger loved it. "I was right there," he said. Television loved it. Ratings for The Open in the US were up 38 per cent over 2017. The fans loved it. Attendance was the largest for any Championship ever held at Carnoustie. Even the other pros loved it. "It's good to have him back," Rory McIlroy insisted. "Good for golf."

Saturday was a surprise. "I didn't know I was tied for the lead," he said. But there he was sharing first place, if briefly, in the third round. "It didn't feel any different to be next to the lead and knowing what I have to do. I've done it so many times."

Not even Tiger would have made that prediction, although he did tell us before the week began if he were going to be a factor in any major it would be The Open, where the ball rolls on linksland fairways and he could be competitive. Was he ever.

Six birdies in all, three, thrillingly, in a row from the ninth. "I had to stay within reach," he said. He did, with an important par at the last when he might have dropped two shots on the last three holes. "I'm right there," he insisted. "I've got a chance at this."

Back in contention and back smiling.

A chance is all Tiger ever wanted. Go back to the start of the year, the start of his latest comeback, there were no guarantees. "The beginning of the year if they'd have said you're playing for The Open Championship, I would be very lucky to do that," he admitted.

So much had been made about Tiger since he arrived with that explosive triumph in the 1997 Masters. Perhaps too much, but the way he won 14 majors, more than anybody other than the remarkable Jack Nicklaus; the way he broke records and then with that scandal broke hearts, he was a golfer apart. He was "The Man".

He stepped out of the past during this Open, giving the younger pros, like Jordan Spieth, who grew up idolising Woods, a rare chance to go up against the golfer as opposed to the image and legend. He gave the two children, Sam Alexis, 11, and Charlie, nine, Woods had with his ex-wife, Elin Nordegren, the opportunity to experience what it was like in an earlier time when he was virtually unbeatable.

"I told them I tried," said Woods. "And I said, 'Hopefully you're proud of your pops for trying as hard as I did.' They gave me some hugs. It was pretty emotional."

Sunday would be a revelation, no fluke, a champion once more playing like one. Leading The Open. The solo leader, at least for a moment, all alone at the top of the leaderboard as he so often was before.

He didn't win. That would have been too much to ask. As might be understood for a golfer too long away from the tension and torment of being in the

The Open would belong to the man paired with Woods, Francesco Molinari, as if verifying the passing of a torch, that the game which once was Tiger's no longer was his, although a tie for sixth in a field as illustrious as that of The Open was no disgrace.

And here was a Tiger who delightfully was more engaging than in his dominant years, when he could be more than a trifle self-indulgent. He would talk to Serena Williams, who in her comeback after giving birth reached the Wimbledon final a few days before The Open — and lost.

Tiger's children, Sam Alexis and Charlie, look on.

"I'm sure she'll call and talk to me because you've got to put things in perspective," said Woods, referring to Williams. "I know it's going to sting for a little bit here but given where I was to where I am now, I'm blessed."

Bobby Jones told us, "I never learned anything from a match I won," meaning defeat instructs. In his thrilling run at Carnoustie, Tiger learned what he lacked, which wasn't a great deal, perhaps youth.

A putt here, a tee shot there, and for the first time since the 2008 US Open Woods grabs that elusive

It's Francesco for Italy!

By Andy Farrell

So many contenders to choose from, so many could have, would have and should haves, but there can only ever be one Champion Golfer of the Year.

On a day when The 147th Open looked to be heading for a play-off — the fourth in a row at Carnoustie — featuring as many as five, six or even seven players, for a winner to emerge in regulation time required an exceptional performance.

To win by two clear strokes from a leaderboard packed with multiple major champions, playing alongside one of the modern greats on this fiery links and to take the Claret Jug back to Italy for the first time, all this made for a special moment in the game of golf.

It turned out not just anyone could achieve all this. On this final day of this thrilling week, during the long, hot summer of 2018, it could only be achieved by Francesco Molinari.

The winning habit came later to the 35-year-old

A moment to savour for a Champion Golfer and his country.

from Turin, but a third victory in six tournaments — plus two runner-up finishes — was acknowledgement that the best player of the moment had won out. All afternoon players got stuck in the revolving door at the top of the leaderboard but only Molinari passed through without being flung back down.

We started with the three overnight leaders, saw Tiger Woods, a decade on from the 14th and last of his previous major victories, take the solo lead for the first time on a Sunday in a major for seven years. When he stumbled, there was a five-way tie at the top — before there were two and then two finally became one.

Molinari produced the sort of final round not seen at The Open since Nick Faldo at Muirfield in 1987. Par after par he made, but that was not going to be good enough. Two late birdies were required to finish two ahead of Justin Rose, Rory McIlroy, Kevin Kisner and Xander Schauffele. Woods tied for sixth place with Eddie Pepperell and Kevin Chappell, while Jordan Spieth, the defending Champion and co-leader after 54 holes with Kisner and Schauffele, dropped down to ninth with Matt Kuchar and Tony Finau.

EXCERPTS FROM THE PRESS

"Francesco Molinari is the first Italian to win a major: he succeeded in The 147th Open, the most ancient and prestigious tournament in the history of this sport, the one that guarantees a direct pass to becoming a legend. From the theatre of nightmares, the fearful course of Carnoustie became for a day the stage of dreams. But only those of Chicco."
—Valentina Buzzi,
La Gazzetta dello Sport

"Somebody once said that Carnoustie was all about gorse management. So it was just as well that David Dawson, a local member, was standing next to one of these hedges from hell when Spieth planted his ball in the middle of it, and it took all his years of hard-won, bitter, prickly experience to help the American to find it."
—Alasdair Reid,
The Times

"Even the greats have to learn to be great again and that goes for Rory McIlroy after he came up two strokes short in his bid for that elusive fifth major. Rather than look back on his turgid start, he felt he didn't so much lose The Open but that Francesco Molinari just went out and won it."
—Brian Keogh,
Irish Independent

Playing in front of a huge gallery was another challenge Molinari overcame.

"I am incredibly proud of what I've done today," said Molinari, clutching the Claret Jug. "I knew I was coming in playing some good golf but I had a terrible record here. Playing with Tiger was another challenge because of the crowds and everything but I felt I was ready for the challenge, and to go bogey-free over the weekend, it's unthinkable. Look at the names on the Claret Jug, they are the best golfers in history. For someone like me, coming from Italy, not really a golfing country, it's been an incredible journey."

Molinari was 12 when he watched with his brother Edoardo, two years the elder, as Costantino Rocca holed a miraculous putt from the Valley of Sin at St Andrews in 1995 before losing in a play-off to John Daly. "I remember the joy when he holed the putt and I remember I was in tears when he lost the play-off," Molinari recalled.

"I hope there were a lot of young kids in Italy watching today and they will be inspired as I was watching Costantino. He is my idol and I hope I made him proud and a lot of other Italians too."

Rocca was playing alongside Woods in the final round of the 1997 Masters when Tiger won his first major. But may it never be forgotten, Rocca defeated Woods in the singles of that year's Ryder Cup. Molinari has twice played Woods in Ryder Cup singles action, earning a vital half at Medinah in 2012, two years after he lined up

Justin Rose closed with a 69 to set the clubhouse target at six-under-par.

After an early wobble, Kevin Kisner kept going to finish as one of the four joint runners-up, his best major result.

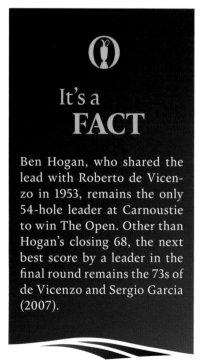

with Edoardo at Celtic Manor — accompanied by the chant: "Two Molinaris, there's only two Molinaris."

Edoardo initially claimed the Molinari spotlight as the 2005 US Amateur champion — and Francesco caddied for him when he played alongside Woods in the Masters the following year — but injuries have held back his career in recent times. "A part of this victory is for him," Francesco said of his brother. "I hope it helps motivate him to get back to where he should be. There are not that many people playing golf in Italy and we pushed each other all the time to get better."

Molinari won the Italian Open in 2006 and his national championship for a second time in 2016 but only two other titles in between. "I probably should have won more in my career but golf is a tough game, everything has to be in place," he said.

Long-term swing coach Denis Pugh has only ever had to fine-tune a high-performance engine worthy of the Ferrari stamp. But Molinari's short game and putting too often failed to pass muster so Phil Kenyon, a putting coach, and Dave Alred, who describes

Rory McIlroy joyfully celebrates holing from 55 feet for an eagle at the 14th, which briefly tied him for the lead.

After a birdie at the first hole, Tommy Fleetwood was disappointed to bogey the fifth and then take seven at the sixth.

A par on the ninth helped Kisner to settle down.

himself as a performance coach, joined the team. Woods, for one, saw the results of the overhaul during their final round at Carnoustie.

"He chipped beautifully," Woods said. "I know he made a couple of putts here and there for par, but to get it where it was basically a kick-in from some of the spots he put himself, that was impressive. Great touch. He was working the ball around the greens. He hit a couple with cut spins, a couple with draw spin. That was cool to see."

Over the last 37 holes at Carnoustie, Molinari made eight birdies and 29 pars. He also did not drop a shot over the weekend when he won the BMW PGA Championship at Wentworth in May. McIlroy is the only other player to do the British double of Open and PGA titles in the same season and had played alongside the Italian at Wentworth. "He didn't miss a shot," McIlroy recalled. "He's always been a great player. With how he has been playing this year, there's maybe just a little more

Round of the Day: Francesco Molinari – 69

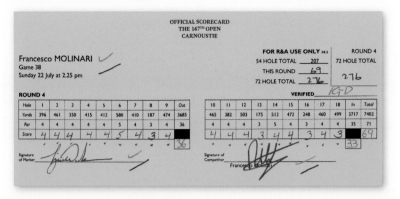

Molinari plays his second shot at the difficult 12th hole, where a four kept his par streak alive.

At the fifth hole, Xander Schauffele gets the close-up treatment from the bunker cam, later checked by a technician.

belief. He's a great guy, this is very well deserved. There's going to be a lot of Europeans vying for his partnership in the foursomes at the Ryder Cup, that's for sure."

Spieth, who in attempting to defend his title did not make a birdie on Sunday, simply marvelled: "Yesterday wasn't too hard not to make a bogey but today was pretty ridiculous. He's been playing unbelievable golf. He's been working his butt off. I see him in the gym all the time, grinding on the range. It truly is hard work that has paid off for Francesco."

Eddie Pepperell birdies the 17th on the way to a 67 and the early clubhouse lead.

For the first time in the week, a respectable Carnoustie breeze of over 20mph ramped up the difficulty factor. Before Spieth and his co-leaders had got fully into their rounds, Pepperell posted the best score of the day, a 67 that left him at five-under-par.

He was still four back but stranger things have happened. In 1999 Paul Lawrie, from 10 behind, closed with a 67 and ended up in a play-off. Lawrie had won the Qatar Masters in windy Doha earlier that season, as had Pepperell this year. The 27-year-old from Oxford was not going anywhere now. "Only because it is Carnoustie and the last four holes, anything can happen, even though they are downwind, with the pressure obviously … So I'll hang around, but if I finish top five, then I'll be delighted." It turned out to be a tie for sixth, not so bad.

Kisner, the leader all week, was the first to wobble. He drove into a pot bunker at the second hole and took two to get out. A double-bogey was followed by a bogey at the third. In the last pairing, Spieth and Schauffele each started with four pars but then both had bunker trouble at the fifth and made bogeys.

Spieth cannot repeat miracle of Birkdale

In the final pairing of the final round at The Open for the second year running, Jordan Spieth once more had to call on the services of David Bonsall, Chairman of The R&A's Rules of Golf Committee. This time the procedure for an unplayable lie in a gorse bush on the sixth hole was rather more straightforward than the protracted ruling that occurred on the 13th hole at Royal Birkdale in 2017.

But while a year ago Spieth produced a miracle bogey and a stunning burst of scoring to win the Claret Jug, this time he was left with a cut finger and a double-bogey-seven after three-putting. Nor did the incident spark another thrilling comeback to claim back-to-back titles. The American's closing 76 did not contain a single birdie as he finished tied for ninth.

Spieth said he hit a three-wood from the rough for his second shot at the sixth because

laying up with an iron would have brought a ditch into play. "It was unlucky. It went into the only bush that's over on the right side. If it misses it, I hit the green and have a birdie putt."

Of his disappointment, Spieth added: "I'm fine. When you put yourself in position enough times, it goes your way sometimes and it doesn't go your way sometimes. I never got down on myself, never got angry. I just didn't make a putt today. That's the most comfortable I've felt in a major on a Sunday, but things didn't go my way."

Tony Finau ended a fine week at Carnoustie in the top 10.

They both then drove into rough on the right of the par-five sixth. Schauffele bogeyed but Spieth took a double-bogey to end his hopes of back-to-back titles. His second shot found a gorse bush and, after a penalty drop that was not as complicated as the one at the 13th at Royal Birkdale a year earlier, he three-putted.

Schauffele got into more trouble with the rough at the seventh and had a double-bogey himself. The significance of this was that Woods was now the sole leader of The Open.

Five years since he last seriously challenged for the Claret Jug, Woods had started the final round best of all the contenders. A birdie at the fourth and another at the sixth where he two-putted from long range got him to seven-under-par. He saved par from bunkers at the eighth and ninth holes to go out in 34 and then, after hitting his tee shot into a bunker on the left of the 10th, played the sort of miracle recovery that was familiar from his heyday. He carried the burn in front of the green although,

Spieth's second at the sixth (above) ends in a bush (right).

unlike in his pomp, the birdie putt did not fall.

Nevertheless, with the atmosphere getting ever more frenzied, Woods was now leading by one from Spieth and Molinari. "Clearly, in my group, the attention wasn't really on me, let's put it that way," said the Italian. "If someone was expecting a charge, probably they weren't expecting it from me, but that's the same my whole career. I had played with Tiger before on big occasions so I knew what was coming, I was ready for it.

"There was everything to make someone nervous, playing the last round of a major close to the lead, playing with Tiger, but I focused on my process and on hitting good shots and playing smart golf. I knew the front nine, with today's wind, was mostly into the wind, so pars were great. I was happy with my score."

Pars were working out just fine. Molinari played one of those fine chips at the fifth to two feet, made a five-footer at the sixth after going in two

Kevin Chappell saves par from a bunker on the eighth hole on the way to finishing tied for sixth place.

bunkers and two-putted from long range at the seventh. From three behind he was now one adrift of his playing partner, but after the 11th he was suddenly tied for the lead.

This is where the trouble started for Woods. In the right rough with his tee shot, he then hit into the gallery on the left with his second. It was the third shot that proved his undoing, a high flop that did not reach the green. He took three more to get down for a double-bogey-six. A bogey at the next and his challenge for a 15th major had come to a premature end.

He did birdie the 14th, chipping from over on the fourth green, but could not find another on the way in. He had never won a major from behind and could not here. "I'm a little ticked off at myself for sure," Woods said. "I had a chance to do something on that back nine and didn't do it."

Molinari had his own issues. At the 12th he had a long putt from off the front of the green for his third and got it to six feet before making another good par save. He missed the green at the short 13th and chipped to eight feet and holed that one

too — just when the mounting pressure of holing out for par after par might have taken a toll on a less resilient mind.

"Those were two really big par putts," he conceded. "Dropping shots at those two holes would have made it a lot harder. Then to flush a drive on the 14th fairway was a key moment as well. That turns the hole into a par four."

A wedge from 160 yards to 50 feet and two putts made his first deviation from par a positive one. It also broke him out of a five-way tie at the top of the leaderboard with Spieth, Schauffele, Chappell and McIlroy. Kisner, Pepperell and Rose had been one behind. It was tight but Molinari had edged in front.

The downwind 14th had already seen plenty of drama. Rose, who started from the cut line on the weekend, hit the flagstick with his approach and had only a tap-in for his eagle. Then McIlroy holed from 55 feet for his own three and the atmosphere was electric once again.

With an exquisite approach to three feet, Rose birdied the 18th for the fourth time out of four and

After creating huge excitement, Tiger Woods misses his bogey putt at the 11th and falls out of the lead.

No Claret Jug but no regrets for Rory

Lying within touching distance of the lead after two rounds, Rory McIlroy said he needed to rediscover the impetuosity of youth in order to win a second Claret Jug. "Even if I don't play my best golf and don't shoot the scores I want, I'm going to go down swinging and I'm going to go down giving it my best," he said. "I just need to get back in that mindset."

It may be an old cliché, but for the Northern Irishman attack really does seem to be his best form of defence. In full swing, he bounds down the fairway, Tigger-like and eager to get to the ball.

On a difficult final day for scoring, McIlroy eventually came up just two strokes shy. There were few of the promised fireworks, but an eagle at the par-five 14th, courtesy of a long, curling putt, brought him seriously into contention. He was disappointed not to build on it in a round of 70, but was able to take the positives from finishing joint runner-up while not playing his best golf.

"I have no regrets. I played the way I wanted to play this week and it gives me a lot of encouragement going into the final major of the year," McIlroy said. "I don't really feel like it's a defeat. I feel like it's a good week. One guy out of 156 is going to win. The 155 other guys are going to leave a little disappointed."

Rose birdies the 18th hole for the fourth day running.

a 69 set the new clubhouse mark at six-under-par. McIlroy could not add a birdie on the last four holes and finished on the same mark after a 70. Chappell had a six at the 17th to drop down to five-under-par with Woods and Pepperell. Kisner, who steadied himself after that ugly start, had three birdies and three bogeys the rest of the way to join Rose and McIlroy at six-under-par.

While Spieth could not buy a putt, Schauffele, who had birdied the 10th from six feet, also birdied the 14th to tie Molinari at seven-under-par. "After the double-bogey I had tried to duck my head," said the man from San Diego. "Looking at the board wasn't doing me any good. Every time I looked up there were four, five, six guys in the lead. Chaotic is probably the best way to put it. Jordan and I had got off to a weird start, feeding off each other in the worst possible way. I was just happy to claw my way back into it and have a chance with four holes to play."

Now it was a two-way battle. Molinari parred the 15th, two-putted from just off the green at the 16th, and then at the 17th, the hardest hole on the day as it played back into the wind, hit a wonderful two-iron to the heart of the green and made four there.

Matt Kuchar birdies the seventh during his 72.

Schauffele plays his approach shot at the 18th needing to hole-out to force a play-off with Molinari.

One last fine drive at the 18th for the eventual winner.

Schauffele, just behind, hit a superb tee shot at the 260-yard 16th but missed his birdie putt. There was a total of zero birdies at the hole all day. As the American headed off down the 17th, Molinari was coming up the 18th. A big drive down the right side left only a 115-yard wedge shot which he played beautifully to five feet.

A huge ovation accompanied the Italian onto the green but he tried to put out of his head what holing the putt would mean. There was plenty of time for that after he had made his second birdie of the day, punched the air in celebration and hugged his caddie, Pello Iguaran.

At the 17th, Schauffele came up short and right and faced a chip over the gorse and bunkers. A bogey meant he had to hole his second at the last to tie. Molinari could not watch and took himself off to the putting green. "I felt sick watching on TV," he said. From that quiet spot he heard that Schauffele had failed to match Zander Lombard's eagle from the previous evening.

A par gave Schauffele a share of second place and, like Kisner, a best major finish. "Hats off to Francesco," he said. "When I looked up on 17 and saw he got to minus-eight, that's just incredible golf. It's a bit of a disappointment, but having a chance to win a major, it's going to go into the memory bank as a positive."

Molinari's major debut had been at Carnoustie in 2007 when his week was cut short on Friday. This time he set a new record for the course of 276 and the celebrations carried onto Monday. A flight back home to London on Sunday night was cancelled but the family holiday to the Bahamas was only delayed 24 hours. And the Claret Jug made for an inimitable centrepiece on the dining table.

"I don't think anyone feels too confident when they stand on the first tee at Carnoustie. I'm lost for words really," Molinari said, sounding as dazed and confused at the end as the rest of us. "No, I mean, it's just disbelief."

Believe it. Carnoustie was fun and Italy has its first Champion Golfer of the Year.

Caddie Pello Iguaran embraces the new Champion.

Molinari celebrates his winning putt, but the Italian still had an agonising wait for his victory to be confirmed.

> *The fact that I had a wedge shot for my approach at the last brought back memories for sure. I was thinking, 'Can I do it again?' I very nearly did.*
>
> —Justin Rose

> *I won't lie, I was a little hungover. I had too much to drink last night, as I was so frustrated yesterday. I didn't have that much to drink, actually, I'm just a lightweight.*
>
> —Eddie Pepperell

> *You've got to love The Open. It's such a great event and getting bigger all the time. It was a pleasure to play the weekend with a chance. Got to wait a year for another chance.*
>
> —Tommy Fleetwood

> *It was brilliant walking down 18 today. I'll never forget an experience like that.*
>
> —Sam Locke

> *It was a great venue. My first time playing Carnoustie and I can't wait to come back here.*
>
> —Louis Oosthuizen

> *It's nice to come off disappointed, in 25th position in a major, whereas a year ago that would have been a really nice finish.*
>
> —Danny Willett

> *Didn't play very good. Didn't strike it good. Never really felt comfortable. Putted, you know, average.*
>
> —Brooks Koepka

> *I have never played golf in Northern Ireland, so I'm excited for next year. This Championship is always special, but I think it's going to be a special one at Portrush.*
>
> —Henrik Stenson

FOURTH ROUND LEADERS

HOLE	1	2	3	4	5	6	7	8	9	10	11	12	13	14	15	16	17	18	TOTAL
PAR	4	4	4	4	4	5	4	3	4	4	4	4	3	5	4	3	4	4	TOTAL
Francesco Molinari	4	4	4	4	4	5	4	3	4	4	4	4	3	4	4	3	4	3	69-276
Justin Rose	4	4	4	4	5	5	4	3	4	4	4	4	3	3	4	3	4	3	69-278
Rory McIlroy	4	5	4	4	5	5	4	3	3	4	3	5	3	3	4	3	4	4	70-278
Kevin Kisner	4	6	5	4	4	4	5	4	4	3	4	5	3	4	4	3	4	4	74-278
Xander Schauffele	4	4	4	4	5	6	6	3	4	3	4	4	3	4	4	3	5	4	74-278
Eddie Pepperell	4	4	3	4	3	4	4	4	4	4	4	4	3	4	4	3	3	4	67-279
Tiger Woods	4	4	4	3	4	4	4	3	4	4	6	5	3	4	4	3	4	4	71-279
Kevin Chappell	5	4	4	4	4	6	4	3	3	4	4	4	3	5	4	3	6	3	73-279

■ EAGLE OR BETTER　■ BIRDIES　□ PAR　■ OVER PAR

SCORING SUMMARY

FOURTH ROUND SCORES

Players Under Par	14
Players At Par	13
Players Over Par	52

CHAMPIONSHIP SCORES

Rounds Under Par	124
Rounds At Par	70
Rounds Over Par	275

LOW SCORES

Low First Nine

Ross Fisher	34
Masahiro Kawamura	34
Brooks Koepka	34
Eddie Pepperell	34
Henrik Stenson	34
Julian Suri	34
Tiger Woods	34

Low Second Nine

Pat Perez	32
Justin Rose	32

Low Round

Eddie Pepperell	67

FOURTH ROUND HOLE SUMMARY

HOLE	PAR	YARDS	EAGLES	BIRDIES	PARS	BOGEYS	D.BOGEYS	OTHER	RANK	AVERAGE
1	4	396	0	7	57	14	0	1	9	4.139
2	4	461	0	11	51	14	3	0	T11	4.114
3	4	350	0	7	58	12	2	0	T11	4.114
4	4	415	0	7	61	11	0	0	15	4.051
5	4	412	0	15	49	14	1	0	16	4.013
6	5	580	1	12	44	16	6	0	8	5.177
7	4	410	0	4	56	16	2	1	6	4.241
8	3	187	0	2	56	19	2	0	T4	3.266
9	4	474	0	7	48	19	5	0	3	4.278
OUT	36	3,685	1	72	480	135	21	2		37.392
10	4	465	0	13	54	11	1	0	17	4.000
11	4	382	0	8	55	14	2	0	10	4.127
12	4	503	0	5	49	24	1	0	T4	4.266
13	3	175	0	4	56	19	0	0	7	3.190
14	5	513	3	58	16	1	1	0	18	4.228
15	4	472	0	7	59	12	1	0	13	4.089
16	3	248	0	0	49	27	3	0	2	3.418
17	4	460	0	3	44	27	5	0	1	4.430
18	4	499	0	15	44	19	1	0	14	4.076
IN	35	3,717	3	113	426	154	15	0		35.823
TOTAL	71	7,402	4	185	906	289	36	2		73.215

An Italian fan salutes the new Champion Golfer of the Year, who posed with the Claret Jug with his wife, Valentina.

CHAMPIONSHIP HOLE SUMMARY

HOLE	PAR	YARDS	EAGLES	BIRDIES	PARS	BOGEYS	D.BOGEYS	OTHER	RANK	AVERAGE
1	4	396	1	53	344	65	4	2	12	4.053
2	4	461	0	64	283	108	14	0	T6	4.154
3	4	350	0	66	338	59	6	0	14	4.011
4	4	415	0	81	326	59	3	0	16	3.966
5	4	412	0	64	318	79	6	2	11	4.070
6	5	580	8	142	232	63	21	3	17	4.908
7	4	410	0	44	333	78	9	5	8	4.147
8	3	187	0	40	326	94	9	0	T6	3.154
9	4	474	0	50	290	115	13	1	5	4.200
OUT	**36**	**3,685**	**9**	**604**	**2,790**	**720**	**85**	**13**		**36.663**
10	4	465	0	65	302	86	15	1	10	4.115
11	4	382	0	96	299	67	7	0	15	3.968
12	4	503	0	19	258	167	23	2	1	4.426
13	3	175	0	68	327	73	1	0	13	3.015
14	5	513	31	279	133	22	4	0	18	4.337
15	4	472	0	41	328	92	8	0	9	4.143
16	3	248	0	20	281	150	16	2	2	3.358
17	4	460	0	26	295	131	17	0	3	4.296
18	4	499	1	63	271	102	23	9	4	4.237
IN	**35**	**3,717**	**32**	**677**	**2,494**	**890**	**114**	**14**		**35.896**
TOTAL	**71**	**7,402**	**41**	**1,281**	**5,284**	**1,610**	**199**	**27**		**72.559**

Francesco's victory was Faldo-esque

Attention to detail the key to exceptional performance, says John Hopkins

The cat was let out of the bag at the 2017 US Open. Francesco Molinari, the younger of the Molinari brothers who have played on the European Tour for more than a decade and the man who would become the 2018 Champion Golfer of the Year, was seen working with Dave Alred.

An Englishman known for coaching Jonny Wilkinson, the rugby player, Alred has also worked in golf with Luke Donald, back when Donald was topping the money lists on both the US and European sides of the Atlantic.

On the first hole at Erin Hills, Molinari was chipping to a flag he could only half see because it was well above his feet. Alred shouted back how close each ball was — 10 feet, six feet, 15 feet and so on — and jotted down the results in a notebook. The two did the same thing on the second hole and the third.

It was an impressive and time consuming display of attention to detail. That was Alred's hallmark when he worked with Wilkinson. He made the rugby player pick out one face in the crowd, out of the hundreds facing him when he was taking an important place kick, and concentrate on that face to the exclusion of all else. What Alred taught Donald was to practise with a purpose and to make every shot count.

"How much of what you do when you prepare is relevant to what you're going to do under pressure," Alred, who has a PhD in sports psychology from Loughborough University, said in an interview in a Sunday newspaper on the eve of The Open. "There is an argument that if a game is unpredictable ... then the practice should be unpredictable. It's very difficult to make yourself uncomfortable. If you surrender what you're doing to somebody else and they make it unpredictable then you put yourself

into discomfort, particularly mentally. That is going to put you in a much better place to perform."

Francesco, the younger by 21 months of the two brothers who are sons of a dentist in Turin, has become a byword for consistency. "Played with Frankie a few weeks ago and couldn't believe how well and accurately the ball was struck," tweeted Eddie Pepperell on the eve of The Open. He was probably the most in-form golfer in the field at Carnoustie having won twice and come second twice in his past five starts.

But that didn't prevent people on hearing that Francesco went for his last 37 holes at Carnoustie without a bogey from admitting to finding that statistic to be astonishing. "That is one of the greatest displays I have seen," Colin Montgomerie said. "Flawless is the word. That is Faldo-esque golf and that is the highest compliment I can pay him. It was a super performance by a lovely guy."

Of the brothers, Edoardo, as well as being the older, is the more talkative, the more demonstrative, the one who lives in Italy. He won the 2005 US Amateur, the first man from Europe to do so since 1911. Franco has a deep voice, does not sound Italian, is not demonstrative, lives in London and became the first Italian to win the Italian Open twice. His nickname for his older brother when they were growing up was "Dodo" because he couldn't pronounce Edoardo.

Molinari's performance was all the more impressive because he did it while playing alongside Tiger Woods on Sunday — and the fans had eyes only for the former world number one. Woods was the epicentre of a storm and poor Molinari should have been right there too. But he wasn't. There was hardly a shout for him, not much applause.

A typical example came on the fourth, the 415-yard hole known as Hillocks. A birdie from Woods gave his supporters the first opportunity to open their lungs in support of him. As his second shot screamed through the wind, the shouts of approval started at the green and rolled back down the fairway to where Woods was disassembling himself after his swing and Molinari was going about his own business.

After the hubbub had died down, a lone voice broke the hush with his own interjection: "Yeah Tiger." Even though Molinari was playing metronomic golf, one par after another, he had to accept that all the noise was for Woods. Until the 18th hole of course. Then the ovation was for Molinari and entirely befitting how the new Champion Golfer had played. How sweet that must have sounded.

What Molinari did on Sunday 22 July was to perform to an exceptional level. The Italian did it so well there were those in golf who wondered why it had taken so long?

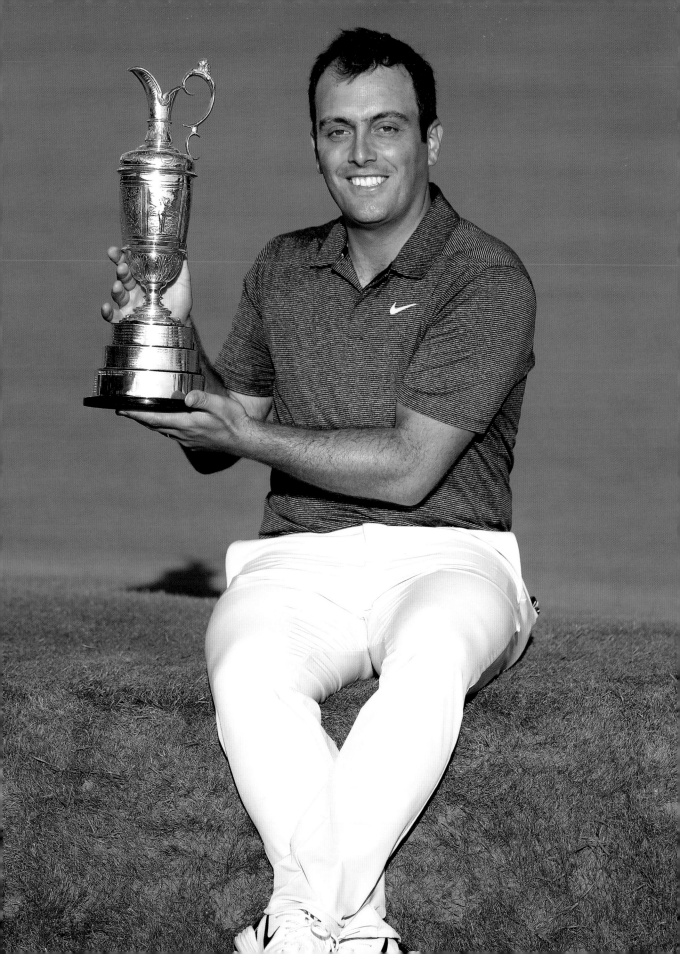

The 147th Open

Complete Scores

Carnoustie Golf Links, Carnoustie, Scotland　　　　　　　　19-22 July 2018

HOLE			1	2	3	4	5	6	7	8	9	10	11	12	13	14	15	16	17	18			
PAR	POS		4	4	4	4	4	5	4	3	4	4	4	4	3	5	4	3	4	4		TOTAL	
Francesco Molinari	T18	Rd 1	3	4	5	3	4	4	4	3	4	5	4	4	2	5	3	4	5	4	70		
Italy	T29	Rd 2	4	3	4	4	4	4	4	3	4	5	3	4	4	4	5	3	6	4	72		
$1,890,000	5	Rd 3	3	4	4	4	4	4	3	3	4	3	4	3	4	4	2	4	4	4	65		
	1	Rd 4	4	4	4	4	4	5	4	3	4	4	4	3	4	4	3	4	3	69	-8	**276**
Justin Rose	T50	Rd 1	4	4	4	4	3	5	5	3	4	4	4	4	3	7	4	3	4	3	72		
England	T65	Rd 2	4	4	4	5	4	5	4	3	4	5	4	4	4	5	4	3	4	3	73		
$694,250	T13	Rd 3	3	4	4	4	4	4	4	3	4	3	4	2	4	4	3	3	3	64		
	T2	Rd 4	4	4	4	4	5	5	4	3	4	4	4	3	3	4	3	4	3	69	-6	**278**
Rory McIlroy	T8	Rd 1	4	4	3	4	5	5	4	3	4	4	4	3	3	4	4	3	4	4	69		
Northern Ireland	T6	Rd 2	4	4	4	4	4	5	3	3	4	3	4	5	2	4	5	3	4	4	69		
$694,250	T6	Rd 3	4	4	4	5	4	4	3	3	4	3	5	3	4	3	4	4	5	70		
	T2	Rd 4	4	5	4	4	5	5	4	3	3	4	3	5	3	3	4	3	4	4	70	-6	**278**
Kevin Kisner	1	Rd 1	4	4	4	4	5	3	4	2	4	4	4	4	2	4	3	3	4	4	66		
USA	T1	Rd 2	4	4	4	4	3	5	3	4	3	5	4	2	4	4	3	4	6	70		
$694,250	T1	Rd 3	4	4	3	4	4	4	4	3	4	4	4	3	4	4	3	4	4	68		
	T2	Rd 4	4	6	5	4	4	4	5	4	4	3	4	5	3	4	4	3	4	4	74	-6	**278**
Xander Schauffele	T32	Rd 1	4	4	4	4	4	5	5	3	4	3	4	4	4	4	3	4	4	71		
USA	T3	Rd 2	4	4	4	4	4	4	4	2	5	4	3	4	3	3	4	3	3	4	66		
$694,250	T1	Rd 3	4	5	4	4	3	4	3	3	4	4	4	3	4	3	3	5	3	67		
	T2	Rd 4	4	4	4	4	5	6	6	3	4	3	4	4	3	4	4	3	5	4	74	-6	**278**
Eddie Pepperell	T32	Rd 1	4	5	4	3	4	5	4	3	4	4	4	4	3	4	4	4	4	4	71		
England	T18	Rd 2	4	4	4	4	4	4	4	4	4	5	4	4	3	3	4	3	4	4	70		
$327,000	T36	Rd 3	3	4	4	4	4	5	4	3	4	4	4	3	4	4	4	4	5	71		
	T6	Rd 4	4	4	3	4	3	4	4	4	4	4	4	3	4	4	3	3	4	67	-5	**279**
Tiger Woods	T32	Rd 1	3	4	4	3	4	5	4	3	4	5	3	4	4	5	5	3	4	4	71		
USA	T29	Rd 2	4	5	5	3	3	5	4	3	5	4	3	4	3	4	4	4	4	4	71		
$327,000	T6	Rd 3	4	4	4	3	4	4	4	3	3	3	3	4	4	4	4	4	4	66		
	T6	Rd 4	4	4	4	3	4	4	4	3	4	4	6	5	3	4	4	3	4	4	71	-5	**279**
Kevin Chappell	T18	Rd 1	3	4	4	4	4	5	4	3	3	4	4	5	3	3	5	4	4	4	70		
USA	T11	Rd 2	4	4	3	4	3	5	4	4	4	3	4	3	4	4	3	4	5	69		
$327,000	4	Rd 3	3	3	4	4	6	4	3	5	4	4	3	3	4	4	3	4	3	67		
	T6	Rd 4	5	4	4	4	4	6	4	3	4	3	4	4	3	5	4	3	6	3	73	-5	**279**

(a) Denotes amateur

HOLE			1	2	3	4	5	6	7	8	9	10	11	12	13	14	15	16	17	18			TOTAL
PAR	POS		4	4	4	4	4	5	4	3	4	4	4	3	5	4	3	4	3	4			
Tony Finau	T2	Rd 1	3	3	5	4	4	4	5	3	3	4	4	5	2	4	3	4	4	3	67		
USA	T6	Rd 2	4	3	4	4	4	5	4	3	4	5	4	3	3	4	5	3	4	5	71		
$219,000	T13	Rd 3	4	5	5	3	3	7	4	3	4	4	4	5	3	3	4	3	3	4	71		
	T9	Rd 4	4	4	4	4	4	5	4	4	4	4	4	4	3	4	4	3	4	4	71	-4	**280**
Matt Kuchar	T18	Rd 1	4	4	3	4	4	4	4	3	4	5	4	4	3	4	5	3	4	4	70		
USA	T6	Rd 2	4	4	4	4	4	4	5	3	4	4	4	4	2	4	4	3	4	3	68		
$219,000	T6	Rd 3	4	3	4	5	5	5	4	4	4	4	3	4	3	4	4	2	4	4	70		
	T9	Rd 4	5	4	5	4	3	5	3	4	4	4	5	3	4	4	4	3	4	4	72	-4	**280**
Jordan Spieth	T50	Rd 1	4	3	4	3	4	5	4	3	4	4	3	4	3	5	6	4	4	5	72		
USA	T11	Rd 2	4	4	3	4	3	5	4	3	4	3	3	4	3	4	4	4	4	4	67		
$219,000	T1	Rd 3	2	4	4	3	4	5	4	3	4	4	3	4	3	4	2	4	4		65		
	T9	Rd 4	4	4	4	4	5	7	4	3	4	4	4	4	3	5	5	3	5	4	76	-4	**280**
Patrick Cantlay	T18	Rd 1	4	4	4	4	3	4	5	3	4	3	4	5	2	4	4	3	4	6	70		
USA	T18	Rd 2	4	4	4	4	4	5	4	3	4	5	3	5	2	4	4	3	5	4	71		
$154,500	T28	Rd 3	4	3	3	3	4	5	3	3	5	4	4	5	3	4	6	3	3	5	70		
	T12	Rd 4	4	4	4	3	4	5	4	3	4	4	4	3	5	4	3	5	3		70	-3	**281**
Thorbjørn Olesen	T18	Rd 1	4	4	4	4	4	4	4	4	3	4	4	4	3	5	3	3	4	5	70		
Denmark	T14	Rd 2	4	4	3	4	4	5	3	3	4	4	4	5	2	4	5	3	5	4	70		
$154,500	T20	Rd 3	4	4	5	3	4	4	3	5	4	5	4	3	3	3	3	4	5		70		
	T12	Rd 4	3	3	4	4	4	5	4	3	6	4	5	5	3	4	4	3	3	4	71	-3	**281**
Ryan Moore	T5	Rd 1	4	3	4	3	3	4	5	2	5	4	4	5	3	5	4	2	4	4	68		
USA	T18	Rd 2	4	4	3	4	4	5	4	3	4	6	4	5	3	5	3	4	4	4	73		
$154,500	T20	Rd 3	5	4	4	3	4	5	4	3	3	4	3	4	4	4	4	4	4	3	69		
	T12	Rd 4	5	3	4	5	4	5	4	3	4	4	4	3	4	3	3	4	5		71	-3	**281**
Tommy Fleetwood	T50	Rd 1	4	3	4	4	5	5	4	3	4	4	4	4	2	5	4	4	5	4	72		
England	T3	Rd 2	4	4	4	3	3	5	4	3	3	4	3	4	3	4	4	3	4	3	65		
$154,500	T6	Rd 3	4	3	4	4	4	6	4	3	4	4	3	6	4	4	3	4	3	4	71		
	T12	Rd 4	3	4	4	4	5	7	5	3	4	4	4	4	3	4	3	4	4	4	73	-3	**281**
Webb Simpson	T18	Rd 1	4	4	4	4	4	5	4	3	4	4	4	5	3	3	4	3	4	4	70		
USA	T18	Rd 2	4	4	4	4	3	5	4	3	4	4	4	4	3	6	4	3	3	5	71		
$154,500	T6	Rd 3	4	4	4	4	4	4	3	3	4	4	4	4	3	4	3	3	4	4	67		
	T12	Rd 4	4	4	5	4	4	5	4	3	5	4	4	5	3	4	4	3	4	4	73	-3	**281**
Jason Day	T32	Rd 1	4	4	4	4	4	4	4	3	4	4	5	5	2	5	4	3	4	4	71		
Australia	T29	Rd 2	4	3	4	4	4	4	4	3	4	3	4	5	3	4	5	4	4	5	71		
$109,714	T51	Rd 3	4	4	4	4	5	5	4	3	3	4	4	6	3	3	4	3	4	5	72		
	T17	Rd 4	4	5	3	4	3	5	4	3	4	4	4	4	2	4	3	3	4	5	68	-2	**282**
Pat Perez	T8	Rd 1	4	3	4	3	4	5	4	3	4	3	5	4	3	4	4	4	4	4	69		
USA	T3	Rd 2	4	4	3	4	4	5	4	2	4	4	3	4	3	4	4	3	4	5	68		
$109,714	T28	Rd 3	4	5	4	3	3	6	3	3	5	4	4	5	3	5	4	4	6	3	74		
	T17	Rd 4	4	4	4	4	4	6	4	5	4	4	4	3	3	4	3	3	5	3	71	-2	**282**
Erik van Rooyen	T2	Rd 1	3	3	4	4	4	4	4	3	4	4	4	3	4	3	5	3	4	5	67		
South Africa	T6	Rd 2	4	5	3	4	4	5	3	3	5	5	3	4	3	5	4	3	4	4	71		
$109,714	T13	Rd 3	4	4	3	4	4	5	4	3	4	3	4	5	4	4	4	4	5	3	71		
	T17	Rd 4	3	3	4	4	4	6	4	3	6	4	5	4	4	4	4	4	4	3	73	-2	**282**
Charley Hoffman	T32	Rd 1	4	5	3	5	3	5	3	4	4	5	4	3	3	5	4	3	4	4	71		
USA	T18	Rd 2	4	3	4	4	4	5	4	4	4	4	4	5	3	4	4	2	4	4	70		
$109,714	T13	Rd 3	4	4	4	3	3	4	4	3	4	4	3	5	3	5	4	3	4	4	68		
	T17	Rd 4	5	3	4	5	5	5	4	4	4	4	4	4	3	4	4	4	4	3	73	-2	**282**

HOLE			1	2	3	4	5	6	7	8	9	10	11	12	13	14	15	16	17	18		
PAR	POS		4	4	4	4	4	5	4	3	4	4	4	4	3	5	4	3	4	4		TOTAL
Adam Scott	T32	Rd 1	4	4	3	4	4	4	4	3	4	4	5	4	3	5	5	3	5	3	71	
Australia	T18	Rd 2	5	3	5	4	4	4	4	2	4	5	3	4	3	4	5	3	4	4	70	
$109,714	T13	Rd 3	4	3	4	4	4	4	4	3	4	3	5	5	3	4	4	2	4	4	68	
	T17	Rd 4	4	4	6	4	5	5	4	4	4	3	4	4	3	4	4	4	4	3	73	-2 **282**
Zach Johnson	T8	Rd 1	4	3	4	4	4	3	4	4	5	5	4	4	3	4	4	3	4	3	69	
USA	T1	Rd 2	5	4	3	3	4	4	4	3	4	4	4	4	3	4	4	3	4	3	67	
$109,714	T6	Rd 3	4	4	4	5	4	3	3	3	4	4	5	6	3	4	4	3	5	4	72	
	T17	Rd 4	5	4	4	4	5	5	4	3	5	3	4	5	3	4	4	3	5	4	74	-2 **282**
Alex Noren	T18	Rd 1	3	5	4	4	4	4	4	3	4	4	3	4	3	5	5	4	3	4	70	
Sweden	T18	Rd 2	4	5	4	4	4	5	4	4	4	4	4	4	3	4	4	2	4	4	71	
$109,714	T6	Rd 3	3	4	4	4	4	4	4	2	5	3	5	4	2	4	4	3	3	5	67	
	T17	Rd 4	4	4	4	4	6	5	4	4	3	4	3	4	4	5	4	3	5	4	74	-2 **282**
Stewart Cink	T50	Rd 1	5	5	5	4	4	3	4	3	5	3	4	4	3	5	4	3	4	4	72	
USA	T29	Rd 2	4	5	4	4	3	5	4	3	4	4	4	4	3	5	4	3	4	3	70	
$84,000	T40	Rd 3	3	5	4	3	5	5	4	3	5	4	4	5	2	4	4	3	4	4	71	
	T24	Rd 4	4	4	3	4	4	6	4	3	3	3	5	5	3	4	4	3	5	3	70	-1 **283**
Phil Mickelson	T72	Rd 1	4	4	4	3	5	5	4	3	4	4	4	5	3	4	4	5	4	4	73	
USA	T29	Rd 2	4	3	4	3	3	7	4	4	4	4	3	4	2	5	4	3	4	4	69	
$84,000	T36	Rd 3	4	4	4	4	3	6	4	3	5	4	4	4	3	4	3	2	5	4	70	
	T24	Rd 4	4	3	4	4	5	5	4	4	3	4	3	4	3	4	4	4	4	5	71	-1 **283**
Bernhard Langer	T72	Rd 1	4	4	4	4	4	6	4	3	3	4	4	4	3	5	4	4	5	4	73	
Germany	T52	Rd 2	4	4	3	4	4	5	5	3	4	4	3	4	4	4	4	4	4	4	71	
$84,000	T36	Rd 3	3	4	4	4	4	4	4	3	5	4	4	5	3	3	4	3	3	4	68	
	T24	Rd 4	4	4	4	4	3	5	5	3	4	4	5	4	3	4	4	3	4	4	71	-1 **283**
Danny Willett	T8	Rd 1	5	4	4	3	3	4	4	3	4	3	4	4	2	5	4	3	5	5	69	
England	T14	Rd 2	3	4	4	4	4	6	4	3	4	4	4	6	3	4	3	3	4	4	71	
$84,000	T20	Rd 3	4	4	4	4	4	5	4	3	4	4	3	5	3	4	4	3	5	3	70	
	T24	Rd 4	4	4	4	5	4	6	4	4	3	4	5	4	2	4	4	3	4	5	73	-1 **283**
Thomas Pieters	T18	Rd 1	3	4	6	4	4	5	4	3	4	3	4	4	3	4	3	3	4	5	70	
Belgium	T40	Rd 2	4	5	4	4	4	5	4	3	4	3	3	5	3	4	4	4	5	5	73	
$67,143	T40	Rd 3	6	4	4	5	3	4	4	3	5	4	3	4	2	4	4	3	4	4	70	
	T28	Rd 4	4	4	4	4	4	5	4	3	5	4	4	4	4	4	3	3	5	3	71	E **284**
Julian Suri	T90	Rd 1	4	5	4	4	4	5	4	3	5	5	4	5	3	4	4	3	4	4	74	
USA	T40	Rd 2	4	4	4	4	4	4	3	3	4	5	3	5	3	4	5	3	4	3	69	
$67,143	T40	Rd 3	4	3	5	4	4	5	4	2	5	4	4	5	2	4	4	3	4	4	70	
	T28	Rd 4	3	4	4	4	3	5	3	3	5	5	3	4	3	4	4	3	6	5	71	E **284**
Patrick Reed	T110	Rd 1	4	6	4	4	5	4	4	3	4	4	4	4	3	5	4	4	4	5	75	
USA	T65	Rd 2	4	4	3	4	3	5	4	3	4	4	3	4	3	4	6	4	4	4	70	
$67,143	T40	Rd 3	4	4	4	4	3	4	3	3	4	4	4	4	2	4	4	4	5	4	68	
	T28	Rd 4	3	4	4	4	4	4	4	3	5	4	5	4	3	4	4	3	4	5	71	E **284**
Rickie Fowler	T18	Rd 1	4	4	3	4	5	5	4	3	4	3	5	5	3	5	4	3	4	3	70	
USA	T11	Rd 2	3	4	3	3	4	5	4	3	5	5	3	4	3	4	4	4	4	4	69	
$67,143	T36	Rd 3	4	3	4	3	4	8	4	4	4	4	4	5	3	3	4	3	4	5	73	
	T28	Rd 4	4	4	5	4	4	4	5	3	5	3	4	4	4	4	3	3	4	5	72	E **284**
Louis Oosthuizen	T50	Rd 1	4	4	4	4	5	4	4	4	4	4	3	3	4	4	4	4	5	4	72	
South Africa	T29	Rd 2	4	5	4	4	3	5	4	3	4	4	3	5	3	4	5	2	4	4	70	
$67,143	T28	Rd 3	3	4	4	3	4	5	4	4	4	4	4	3	4	3	3	4	4	5	69	
	T28	Rd 4	5	4	4	4	4	4	5	3	5	4	4	5	3	4	4	3	4	4	73	E **284**

HOLE			1	2	3	4	5	6	7	8	9	10	11	12	13	14	15	16	17	18			
PAR	POS		4	4	4	4	5	4	3	4	4	4	4	3	5	4	3	4	4	4			TOTAL
Chris Wood	T18	Rd 1	4	4	4	4	5	4	5	3	4	3	3	5	3	5	4	3	4	3	70		
England	T52	Rd 2	4	5	4	5	4	5	4	3	4	4	4	4	3	4	4	4	4	5	74		
$67,143	T20	Rd 3	3	4	3	4	3	4	3	3	4	3	4	4	2	6	4	3	5	4	66		
	T28	Rd 4	4	4	4	4	4	5	4	3	4	5	4	5	4	4	4	3	5	4	74	E	**284**
Austin Cook	T50	Rd 1	4	4	3	4	6	5	4	4	4	3	3	4	4	4	4	3	5	4	72		
USA	T29	Rd 2	4	5	4	4	3	5	4	4	4	4	4	3	4	4	4	3	3	4	70		
$67,143	T13	Rd 3	4	3	4	3	4	4	3	4	4	4	4	4	4	4	3	4	4	4	67		
	T28	Rd 4	4	5	4	4	4	7	4	3	5	4	4	4	3	4	4	4	4	4	75	E	**284**
Henrik Stenson	T18	Rd 1	4	4	4	4	4	4	4	4	4	4	4	5	3	4	3	3	4	4	70		
Sweden	T65	Rd 2	4	5	4	5	5	5	4	3	4	4	4	4	4	4	4	3	5	4	75		
$53,750	T61	Rd 3	4	4	5	6	4	4	4	3	3	4	4	4	3	3	4	3	4	5	71		
	T35	Rd 4	4	4	4	3	4	5	3	3	4	4	4	5	3	4	4	3	4	4	69	+1	**285**
Adam Hadwin	T72	Rd 1	4	4	4	4	4	5	4	3	4	5	4	5	2	4	5	4	4	4	73		
Canada	T40	Rd 2	4	5	4	4	4	5	3	4	4	4	4	3	3	4	4	3	4	4	70		
$53,750	T51	Rd 3	4	3	4	4	5	4	4	3	4	4	3	4	3	4	4	3	5	6	71		
	T35	Rd 4	4	4	4	4	4	5	4	3	4	4	4	4	3	4	4	4	4	4	71	+1	**285**
Michael Kim	T72	Rd 1	4	4	5	4	3	5	4	3	4	4	3	4	4	5	4	4	5	4	73		
USA	T29	Rd 2	3	4	4	4	4	5	4	3	4	4	3	5	2	5	4	2	4	5	69		
$53,750	T28	Rd 3	4	4	3	5	3	5	4	3	4	5	3	4	3	4	3	4	4	4	69		
	T35	Rd 4	4	5	4	4	4	5	4	3	4	4	4	3	3	5	4	4	5	5	74	+1	**285**
Satoshi Kodaira	T50	Rd 1	5	5	4	4	5	4	4	3	4	4	2	4	4	4	4	4	4	3	72		
Japan	T40	Rd 2	4	6	4	4	4	4	3	3	5	5	4	4	3	4	4	4	3	3	71		
$53,750	T28	Rd 3	4	4	5	4	3	4	3	2	4	4	4	5	3	3	4	4	4	4	68		
	T35	Rd 4	4	4	4	4	5	5	4	3	5	4	4	4	4	4	4	4	4	4	74	+1	**285**
Luke List	T18	Rd 1	4	4	4	5	5	4	5	3	4	3	4	4	3	4	2	4	4	4	70		
USA	T14	Rd 2	5	4	4	3	4	5	4	3	4	4	4	3	4	4	3	4	4	4	70		
$41,375	T69	Rd 3	4	5	6	4	5	5	4	3	4	4	6	3	4	5	3	5	3	4	77		
	T39	Rd 4	4	3	5	4	3	4	4	4	4	4	4	5	2	4	4	3	4	4	69	+2	**286**
Brooks Koepka	T50	Rd 1	3	4	4	4	6	5	5	5	5	3	4	3	2	4	4	4	3	4	72		
USA	T18	Rd 2	4	4	4	3	4	4	4	3	4	4	5	4	3	4	4	4	4	3	69		
$41,375	T61	Rd 3	4	4	5	4	4	6	4	4	4	3	6	3	4	4	3	5	4	4	75		
	T39	Rd 4	3	4	4	4	5	5	4	2	3	5	4	4	3	4	5	3	5	3	70	+2	**286**
Cameron Davis	T32	Rd 1	4	4	4	3	6	5	4	3	3	5	6	4	2	4	4	3	4	3	71		
Australia	T40	Rd 2	4	3	4	4	4	5	3	4	4	6	3	4	3	5	4	3	5	4	72		
$41,375	T61	Rd 3	4	4	3	4	5	5	4	4	4	4	6	2	4	4	4	4	4	4	73		
	T39	Rd 4	4	3	4	3	5	5	4	4	4	5	3	2	4	5	3	4	5	5	70	+2	**286**
Ryan Fox	T90	Rd 1	4	5	5	4	4	5	5	3	4	4	3	4	3	4	4	4	5	4	74		
New Zealand	T65	Rd 2	4	4	4	4	4	5	4	3	4	4	3	4	3	5	4	3	5	4	71		
$41,375	T61	Rd 3	4	4	4	4	4	5	4	3	4	4	4	3	4	4	3	5	4	4	71		
	T39	Rd 4	4	4	4	4	3	5	4	3	4	4	4	5	3	4	4	3	4	4	70	+2	**286**
Masahiro Kawamura	T137	Rd 1	7	4	4	4	4	4	4	4	5	4	4	3	4	5	3	4	5	5	77		
Japan	T52	Rd 2	4	3	4	4	4	4	4	2	4	4	4	5	3	3	4	3	4	4	67		
$41,375	T56	Rd 3	3	4	3	4	4	5	3	3	5	3	4	5	3	5	5	3	4	5	71		
	T39	Rd 4	4	4	4	3	4	4	4	3	4	5	5	4	3	4	4	3	5	4	71	+2	**286**
Ross Fisher	T110	Rd 1	4	4	4	4	4	4	5	3	5	5	4	4	3	5	4	3	5	5	75		
England	T65	Rd 2	4	4	4	3	4	5	4	4	4	4	3	4	3	4	4	3	4	5	70		
$41,375	T40	Rd 3	4	4	3	4	4	6	4	2	4	3	4	5	3	4	3	3	4	4	68		
	T39	Rd 4	4	5	4	3	4	3	4	3	4	4	4	4	4	5	5	4	5	4	73	+2	**286**

HOLE			1	2	3	4	5	6	7	8	9	10	11	12	13	14	15	16	17	18		
PAR	POS		4	4	4	4	4	5	4	3	4	4	4	4	3	5	4	3	4	4		TOTAL
Kyle Stanley	T50	Rd 1	4	4	5	4	4	4	4	3	4	3	3	5	3	5	4	4	5	4	72	
USA	T18	Rd 2	3	4	4	4	4	5	3	3	3	5	4	4	3	5	4	3	4	4	69	
$41,375	T20	Rd 3	4	4	4	3	5	5	5	3	4	3	3	4	3	4	4	3	5	3	69	
	T39	Rd 4	4	4	3	5	4	5	4	4	5	4	5	5	3	4	4	4	4	5	76	+2 **286**
Haotong Li	T32	Rd 1	3	5	5	3	5	4	5	3	4	4	3	4	3	5	4	4	4	3	71	
China	T40	Rd 2	4	4	3	4	4	4	3	4	5	4	4	4	3	5	4	3	4	6	72	
$41,375	T20	Rd 3	4	4	4	4	3	5	4	3	3	3	4	3	4	4	3	4	4	4	67	
	T39	Rd 4	4	6	5	3	5	5	4	4	5	5	4	3	4	4	4	4	4	3	76	+2 **286**
Brendan Steele	T5	Rd 1	4	4	4	4	5	4	4	3	3	4	3	5	3	4	4	3	3	4	68	
USA	T52	Rd 2	4	4	4	4	4	5	4	4	6	4	4	4	3	5	5	4	4	4	76	
$31,000	T69	Rd 3	4	3	4	5	4	5	4	4	4	3	4	6	3	3	5	4	4	4	73	
	T47	Rd 4	4	4	4	3	4	6	4	3	4	4	4	4	3	4	4	3	4	4	70	+3 **287**
Tom Lewis	T110	Rd 1	4	4	5	5	5	4	4	3	4	4	4	4	3	6	5	3	4	4	75	
England	T65	Rd 2	4	4	3	4	3	5	4	3	3	4	4	4	2	5	4	4	4	6	70	
$31,000	T40	Rd 3	4	3	3	4	4	5	4	3	4	5	3	4	3	4	4	3	4	4	68	
	T47	Rd 4	5	4	4	5	4	4	4	3	4	5	4	4	3	4	3	4	5	5	74	+3 **287**
Sean Crocker	T32	Rd 1	4	3	4	5	5	4	5	3	4	4	3	4	4	4	4	2	4	5	71	
USA	T29	Rd 2	5	4	4	3	4	4	4	4	4	5	4	4	3	4	4	3	4	4	71	
$31,000	T28	Rd 3	3	4	4	4	4	5	3	2	4	4	3	5	4	4	5	3	4	4	69	
	T47	Rd 4	4	5	4	4	4	7	4	3	4	4	4	5	4	4	4	4	4	4	76	+3 **287**
Yusaku Miyazato	T32	Rd 1	5	3	4	4	4	4	2	4	3	4	4	3	7	4	4	4	4	4	71	
Japan	T65	Rd 2	4	4	4	4	3	5	4	4	6	4	4	4	2	3	4	3	5	7	74	
$31,000	T20	Rd 3	4	3	4	3	4	4	4	2	4	4	4	4	3	4	4	3	3	4	65	
	T47	Rd 4	4	5	4	5	4	6	4	3	6	3	4	5	3	5	4	4	5	3	77	+3 **287**
Bryson DeChambeau	T110	Rd 1	4	5	4	4	3	4	3	6	5	4	5	3	5	5	3	4	4	75		
USA	T65	Rd 2	4	3	3	4	4	6	4	4	4	5	4	3	2	5	4	4	4	3	70	
$27,161	T74	Rd 3	4	3	5	5	4	4	4	4	4	4	5	4	2	4	4	4	4	5	73	
	T51	Rd 4	5	3	4	4	3	5	4	3	4	4	4	4	4	4	4	3	4	4	70	+4 **288**
Tyrrell Hatton	T90	Rd 1	4	4	5	4	5	6	5	3	4	4	4	4	3	5	4	3	4	3	74	
England	T65	Rd 2	4	6	4	4	4	4	4	3	4	4	4	4	3	4	4	3	4	4	71	
$27,161	T69	Rd 3	5	4	5	4	4	4	4	3	4	3	4	4	4	4	4	3	4	5	72	
	T51	Rd 4	4	4	4	4	4	5	4	3	4	4	4	4	3	4	4	4	4	4	71	+4 **288**
Kevin Na	T18	Rd 1	4	4	4	4	4	4	6	2	4	4	5	4	3	4	3	3	4	4	70	
USA	T40	Rd 2	4	5	3	5	4	5	4	4	4	4	4	4	3	4	5	3	4	4	73	
$27,161	T61	Rd 3	4	4	4	4	4	5	4	3	5	4	4	4	4	5	4	3	4	4	73	
	T51	Rd 4	4	4	4	5	4	4	5	3	5	3	4	3	4	4	4	3	5	4	72	+4 **288**
Paul Casey	T72	Rd 1	4	5	4	5	4	5	4	3	4	4	4	4	3	4	4	3	5	4	73	
England	T52	Rd 2	4	4	4	4	4	5	4	3	4	5	3	5	3	4	4	3	4	4	71	
$27,161	T61	Rd 3	5	4	4	4	5	4	4	3	4	4	4	5	3	4	3	3	4	5	72	
	T51	Rd 4	4	4	4	4	4	5	5	3	4	4	3	4	4	4	4	4	5	3	72	+4 **288**
Shubhankar Sharma	T72	Rd 1	4	4	4	4	4	5	5	3	4	5	5	5	3	4	4	3	4	4	73	
India	T52	Rd 2	5	4	4	4	4	5	4	4	5	3	4	5	2	4	4	3	4	3	71	
$27,161	T56	Rd 3	4	3	4	4	4	5	4	3	5	5	4	4	3	4	3	4	4	4	71	
	T51	Rd 4	4	4	3	4	3	5	4	4	4	4	5	4	4	5	5	3	4	4	73	+4 **288**
Yuta Ikeda	T18	Rd 1	4	3	5	3	4	4	5	3	5	3	4	4	2	5	5	3	4	4	70	
Japan	T40	Rd 2	4	4	4	4	4	5	4	3	4	5	4	4	3	5	3	3	4	6	73	
$27,161	T51	Rd 3	4	4	5	4	4	5	5	3	4	4	4	4	3	4	3	4	4	3	71	
	T51	Rd 4	4	4	4	4	4	5	5	3	4	4	4	4	3	4	5	3	5	5	74	+4 **288**

HOLE			1	2	3	4	5	6	7	8	9	10	11	12	13	14	15	16	17	18		
PAR	POS		4	4	4	4	4	5	4	3	4	4	4	4	3	5	4	3	4	4	TOTAL	
Jason Dufner	T110	Rd 1	4	4	5	5	4	4	5	4	3	3	5	4	2	4	6	3	6	4	75	
USA	T65	Rd 2	4	4	4	4	4	6	4	3	3	4	5	3	2	5	4	3	4	4	70	
$27,161	T40	Rd 3	4	4	4	4	4	4	4	3	4	4	4	4	3	4	4	3	4	3	68	
	T51	Rd 4	4	4	5	4	4	5	4	4	4	3	3	4	3	5	6	5	4	4	75	+4 288
Lucas Herbert	T72	Rd 1	5	3	4	4	4	4	4	5	4	5	4	5	3	4	4	3	4	4	73	
Australia	T29	Rd 2	4	4	3	4	3	4	4	3	5	4	3	5	3	5	4	3	4	4	69	
$27,161	T28	Rd 3	3	5	4	4	3	4	4	3	5	4	4	5	3	3	4	3	4	4	69	
	T51	Rd 4	4	5	4	4	4	6	4	3	6	4	4	3	4	4	4	3	5	6	77	+4 288
Byeong Hun An	T72	Rd 1	3	3	4	3	4	5	4	3	3	5	4	3	3	4	4	3	4	7	73	
Korea	T52	Rd 2	4	5	4	4	4	5	4	3	4	3	4	4	3	4	4	4	4	4	71	
$27,161	T20	Rd 3	4	4	4	3	3	5	4	3	3	3	3	4	3	5	4	3	4	4	66	
	T51	Rd 4	4	5	5	5	3	5	4	3	4	5	4	4	3	4	5	4	6	5	78	+4 288
Marc Leishman	T50	Rd 1	4	4	3	3	4	4	4	2	5	6	3	5	3	6	4	4	4	4	72	
Australia	T52	Rd 2	4	4	4	3	4	5	5	2	4	4	4	6	3	4	4	4	4	4	72	
$25,800	T40	Rd 3	4	4	5	3	4	4	4	2	4	4	4	4	3	4	4	3	5	4	69	
	60	Rd 4	5	3	4	4	4	6	4	5	5	4	4	5	3	4	4	3	5	4	76	+5 289
Brett Rumford	T90	Rd 1	4	3	4	4	5	4	3	5	3	4	5	3	5	4	4	4	5	5	74	
Australia	T52	Rd 2	4	3	4	4	5	4	3	4	4	4	4	3	5	4	2	4	4	5	70	
$25,317	T61	Rd 3	4	4	5	3	4	4	3	4	5	4	3	5	3	4	5	3	5	4	72	
	T61	Rd 4	5	4	4	4	3	5	5	4	3	3	3	5	4	5	4	3	4	5	74	+6 290
Gavin Green	T50	Rd 1	4	5	4	3	5	4	5	2	4	4	4	5	2	4	4	3	5	5	72	
Malaysia	T65	Rd 2	4	5	3	4	4	5	4	3	4	5	4	4	3	4	5	3	4	5	73	
$25,317	T61	Rd 3	4	4	4	4	4	4	4	4	4	4	3	4	3	6	4	4	4	4	71	
	T61	Rd 4	4	4	4	4	4	7	4	3	4	4	4	4	4	4	4	3	5	4	74	+6 290
Marcus Kinhult	T90	Rd 1	5	4	4	4	4	5	3	3	4	3	4	4	3	4	5	5	4	6	74	
Sweden	T40	Rd 2	4	4	4	3	3	5	4	3	4	4	5	4	3	4	4	3	4	4	69	
$25,317	T51	Rd 3	4	4	4	3	4	5	4	3	5	4	4	5	2	4	4	3	5	4	71	
	T61	Rd 4	4	5	4	5	4	6	4	4	3	4	3	4	3	4	4	4	6	5	76	+6 290
Brandon Stone	T5	Rd 1	4	4	3	4	4	4	4	2	4	4	4	4	3	4	5	3	4	4	68	
South Africa	T14	Rd 2	4	5	3	4	4	5	4	3	4	4	4	5	4	4	4	3	4	4	72	
$25,317	T40	Rd 3	4	4	5	4	4	5	4	3	4	4	5	4	3	5	4	3	4	4	73	
	T61	Rd 4	5	3	4	5	4	5	5	3	4	5	4	4	5	5	4	4	4	4	77	+6 290
Lee Westwood	T50	Rd 1	4	4	4	4	4	5	4	3	5	4	3	5	3	5	4	3	4	4	72	
England	T52	Rd 2	4	5	4	4	4	4	4	3	4	3	4	5	3	3	5	3	5	5	72	
$25,317	T40	Rd 3	4	4	5	4	4	4	4	3	5	4	3	4	3	3	4	3	4	4	69	
	T61	Rd 4	3	5	4	4	4	5	5	3	4	6	5	5	3	5	5	3	4	4	77	+6 290
Shaun Norris	T90	Rd 1	4	4	4	4	4	4	3	4	4	4	4	4	3	6	5	3	5	5	74	
South Africa	T29	Rd 2	4	3	3	4	4	6	4	3	4	3	4	4	3	4	5	3	3	4	68	
$25,317	T28	Rd 3	3	4	4	4	5	3	2	5	6	3	4	4	3	4	4	3	4	4	69	
	T61	Rd 4	8	4	5	4	4	6	3	3	4	5	4	4	3	5	5	3	4	5	79	+6 290
Si Woo Kim	T32	Rd 1	4	4	4	4	5	4	4	3	4	4	5	4	4	4	3	3	4	4	71	
Korea	T40	Rd 2	5	4	4	4	4	4	5	3	3	4	4	5	3	4	4	3	4	5	72	
$24,250	T74	Rd 3	4	5	4	4	4	5	4	3	3	4	5	5	3	4	5	5	4	4	75	
	T67	Rd 4	4	3	4	4	4	5	4	4	4	4	4	4	3	6	4	4	4	4	73	+7 291
Paul Dunne	T32	Rd 1	5	3	4	4	4	5	4	3	5	4	4	3	3	5	4	3	4	4	71	
Republic of Ireland	T52	Rd 2	3	5	4	4	4	4	5	3	4	4	4	4	4	5	5	3	4	4	73	
$24,250	T69	Rd 3	4	4	4	4	4	5	4	4	3	5	4	4	3	5	4	3	3	6	73	
	T67	Rd 4	5	5	3	4	3	5	4	3	5	4	4	5	3	4	4	4	4	5	74	+7 291

HOLE			1	2	3	4	5	6	7	8	9	10	11	12	13	14	15	16	17	18			
PAR	POS		4	4	4	4	4	5	4	3	4	4	4	4	3	5	4	3	4	4			TOTAL
Gary Woodland	T32	Rd 1	4	4	3	3	4	4	5	3	5	6	3	4	4	4	4	3	4	4	71		
USA	T40	Rd 2	4	3	4	4	5	5	3	2	5	4	4	4	3	5	4	4	5	4	72		
$24,250	T56	Rd 3	4	4	4	4	4	5	5	3	4	4	4	4	3	4	5	3	4	4	72		
	T67	Rd 4	4	4	5	4	4	5	4	4	5	4	4	4	4	5	4	4	5	3	76	+7	**291**
Rhys Enoch	T90	Rd 1	4	5	3	4	4	4	4	4	5	4	5	4	4	4	4	4	4	4	74		
Wales	T65	Rd 2	3	4	4	4	4	5	5	2	4	4	4	5	3	5	4	3	4	4	71		
$24,250	T56	Rd 3	4	5	5	3	3	4	5	3	4	5	3	4	2	4	5	3	5	3	70		
	T67	Rd 4	5	4	4	3	6	6	3	4	4	5	3	4	5	3	4	5	4	5	76	+7	**291**
Matthew Southgate	T8	Rd 1	4	5	4	4	4	3	4	3	4	3	3	5	4	3	4	4	4	4	69		
England	T18	Rd 2	6	4	3	4	5	4	4	4	5	4	4	4	3	4	3	3	4	4	72		
$24,250	T51	Rd 3	3	5	4	4	4	6	4	3	4	4	4	4	3	5	3	4	4	5	73		
	T67	Rd 4	4	4	4	4	5	4	5	3	5	4	4	5	3	5	4	4	6	4	77	+7	**291**
Sung Kang	T8	Rd 1	4	3	4	4	4	5	4	3	3	4	4	3	4	4	4	4	4	4	69		
Korea	T18	Rd 2	4	4	3	4	4	5	4	3	5	4	5	4	3	4	5	3	4	4	72		
$24,250	T40	Rd 3	5	4	4	4	5	4	3	3	4	4	5	4	3	3	4	4	5	4	72		
	T67	Rd 4	4	4	5	4	4	6	5	3	4	5	4	5	3	5	4	4	5	4	78	+7	**291**
Zander Lombard	T2	Rd 1	4	3	4	4	3	4	4	2	4	5	4	3	4	4	3	4	4	4	67		
South Africa	T6	Rd 2	4	4	3	4	4	5	3	3	4	4	4	5	3	4	4	4	5	4	71		
$24,250	T13	Rd 3	4	5	4	3	3	5	4	3	4	4	4	4	3	5	4	4	6	2	71		
	T67	Rd 4	4	4	4	4	5	6	5	3	5	4	6	6	3	4	5	5	5	4	82	+7	**291**
Rafa Cabrera Bello	T90	Rd 1	3	4	4	4	5	4	4	3	3	5	4	5	3	4	4	6	4	5	74		
Spain	T52	Rd 2	4	4	4	3	4	5	4	3	5	3	4	5	3	4	4	3	4	4	70		
$23,675	T78	Rd 3	4	3	4	3	4	7	4	3	4	5	4	5	4	6	4	3	5	4	76		
	74	Rd 4	4	4	4	4	5	4	4	3	5	4	4	3	4	4	4	3	5	4	72	+8	**292**
Beau Hossler	T72	Rd 1	3	5	4	4	5	4	4	3	4	4	3	4	3	5	4	3	6	5	73		
USA	T40	Rd 2	4	4	4	4	5	6	4	2	5	3	4	4	3	3	4	3	4	4	70		
$23,488	T78	Rd 3	5	3	4	4	4	5	6	3	4	5	4	5	3	5	4	3	4	6	77		
	T75	Rd 4	4	5	5	4	4	5	5	3	5	3	4	5	3	3	4	3	4	4	73	+9	**293**
Kiradech Aphibarnrat	T90	Rd 1	3	4	6	3	4	5	4	3	4	5	3	5	3	6	4	4	3	4	74		
Thailand	T65	Rd 2	4	4	4	5	4	4	4	3	3	4	4	5	4	4	4	3	4	4	71		
$23,488	77	Rd 3	4	5	5	4	4	4	4	3	5	4	3	6	3	4	4	3	4	5	74		
	T75	Rd 4	4	6	4	5	3	4	4	3	4	3	5	4	3	4	4	5	5	4	74	+9	**293**
Sam Locke [a]	T50	Rd 1	4	4	4	4	5	4	5	2	5	4	4	3	4	4	5	4	4	3	72		
Scotland	T65	Rd 2	4	5	6	4	4	5	4	3	4	4	4	4	2	4	3	4	4	5	73		
	T56	Rd 3	3	4	3	3	4	6	4	2	5	4	4	5	2	6	4	4	4	3	70		
	T75	Rd 4	4	5	4	4	4	5	4	2	4	5	4	5	4	7	4	4	5	4	78	+9	**293**
Cameron Smith	T72	Rd 1	4	4	4	4	5	4	4	4	4	3	5	3	3	4	5	4	5	4	73		
Australia	T52	Rd 2	4	5	4	3	4	5	5	3	4	4	4	4	3	4	4	3	4	4	71		
$23,300	T69	Rd 3	4	4	5	4	4	4	4	3	4	6	3	4	3	4	4	3	5	5	73		
	78	Rd 4	5	4	4	4	4	7	4	3	6	4	5	4	4	4	4	4	3	4	77	+10	**294**
Keegan Bradley	T90	Rd 1	4	4	4	4	4	4	4	5	3	4	4	5	3	4	4	4	5	5	74		
USA	T65	Rd 2	5	4	4	5	4	5	5	2	4	4	4	4	2	4	4	3	3	5	71		
$23,175	T74	Rd 3	4	4	4	5	4	5	4	3	4	4	4	5	3	5	4	4	3	4	73		
	79	Rd 4	4	4	6	4	4	6	7	3	4	4	4	4	3	4	4	3	4	5	77	+11	**295**

NON QUALIFIERS AFTER 36 HOLES
(Leading 10 professionals and ties receive $7,375 each, next 20 professionals and ties receive $5,900 each, remainder of professionals receive $4,950 each.)

HOLE			1	2	3	4	5	6	7	8	9	10	11	12	13	14	15	16	17	18		TOTAL
PAR	POS		4	4	4	4	5	4	3	4	4	4	4	3	5	4	3	4	4			
Daniel Berger	T72	Rd 1	5	4	4	5	4	4	4	3	4	5	3	4	3	4	4	3	5	5	73	
USA	**T80**	Rd 2	3	4	4	4	4	5	4	3	4	4	4	5	2	5	5	4	5	4	73	+4 **146**
Justin Thomas	T8	Rd 1	4	4	3	4	4	4	4	3	3	4	3	5	3	5	4	4	4	4	69	
USA	**T80**	Rd 2	4	4	4	5	3	7	6	5	4	4	4	4	2	4	4	4	5	4	77	+4 **146**
Branden Grace	T90	Rd 1	4	4	4	4	4	6	4	4	4	4	4	4	3	4	5	3	5	4	74	
South Africa	**T80**	Rd 2	4	4	4	4	4	5	3	3	5	5	4	5	2	4	4	3	5	4	72	+4 **146**
Chez Reavie	T8	Rd 1	4	4	4	3	4	5	5	3	4	4	3	4	3	4	4	3	4	4	69	
USA	**T80**	Rd 2	6	4	3	4	4	5	4	3	5	4	5	5	3	6	3	3	5	5	77	+4 **146**
Tom Lehman	T110	Rd 1	4	5	4	4	4	6	4	4	4	4	4	5	3	6	4	3	3	4	75	
USA	**T80**	Rd 2	3	4	4	4	5	4	4	3	4	4	4	5	3	5	3	3	5	4	71	+4 **146**
Matt Wallace	T90	Rd 1	4	4	4	4	5	6	4	4	4	4	4	5	2	4	4	4	4	4	74	
England	**T80**	Rd 2	4	3	4	3	4	5	4	3	6	3	4	5	3	4	4	4	5	4	72	+4 **146**
Sergio Garcia	T110	Rd 1	5	4	5	4	4	4	4	3	5	5	5	5	3	5	4	3	4	3	75	
Spain	**T80**	Rd 2	4	5	4	4	4	5	4	2	4	4	3	5	2	4	4	5	4	4	71	+4 **146**
Hideki Matsuyama	T110	Rd 1	4	5	4	4	5	5	4	4	4	4	5	4	3	4	5	3	4	4	75	
Japan	**T80**	Rd 2	4	4	4	4	3	5	4	3	4	4	5	3	3	4	4	2	4	7	71	+4 **146**
Russell Knox	T72	Rd 1	5	5	4	4	4	4	4	3	5	5	4	4	3	4	3	4	3	5	73	
Scotland	**T80**	Rd 2	4	5	4	4	4	5	5	3	5	4	4	3	4	4	4	3	4	4	73	+4 **146**
Fabrizio Zanotti	T50	Rd 1	5	3	4	5	3	5	4	2	3	4	5	5	4	5	4	4	3	4	72	
Paraguay	**T80**	Rd 2	4	4	3	4	4	5	3	3	5	4	4	5	3	5	4	5	5	4	74	+4 **146**
Martin Kaymer	T32	Rd 1	4	3	4	5	4	4	4	3	5	4	3	4	4	3	4	4	5	4	71	
Germany	**T80**	Rd 2	4	5	4	4	4	6	4	3	3	5	4	5	3	4	4	4	5	4	75	+4 **146**
George Coetzee	T110	Rd 1	4	5	4	3	4	5	4	3	5	4	5	5	3	5	3	5	4	4	75	
South Africa	**T80**	Rd 2	4	4	3	4	5	4	4	3	3	4	4	4	4	5	4	3	4	5	71	+4 **146**
Peter Uihlein	T90	Rd 1	4	5	4	5	4	5	3	3	4	4	6	3	3	5	3	4	5	4	74	
USA	**T80**	Rd 2	3	4	4	4	4	6	5	2	3	4	5	4	3	5	5	3	4	4	72	+4 **146**
Charl Schwartzel	T90	Rd 1	4	5	4	4	4	4	8	2	4	4	5	3	4	3	3	4	4	5	74	
South Africa	**T93**	Rd 2	4	5	4	4	4	4	5	3	4	5	4	4	3	5	5	2	4	4	73	+5 **147**
Kelly Kraft	T90	Rd 1	4	4	4	4	5	5	4	3	4	4	4	3	5	4	5	4	4	4	74	
USA	**T93**	Rd 2	4	6	4	4	3	5	4	4	3	3	3	5	3	5	5	3	5	4	73	+5 **147**
Matthew Fitzpatrick	T50	Rd 1	4	4	4	4	4	4	4	4	4	4	4	4	4	4	5	3	4	4	72	
England	**T93**	Rd 2	4	4	4	4	5	6	3	3	6	5	6	4	2	4	5	3	4	3	75	+5 **147**
Jorge Campillo	T50	Rd 1	4	4	3	4	5	5	5	3	4	4	5	3	4	4	3	5	4	3	72	
Spain	**T93**	Rd 2	5	4	4	3	5	6	4	4	4	5	5	4	2	4	4	3	4	5	75	+5 **147**
Jordan Smith	T90	Rd 1	4	4	4	4	4	4	4	3	3	5	4	5	4	4	5	3	5	5	74	
England	**T93**	Rd 2	3	4	4	4	4	6	4	3	4	4	5	5	2	4	4	3	4	6	73	+5 **147**
Andy Sullivan	T32	Rd 1	3	4	4	3	4	5	5	4	4	4	4	4	4	4	3	4	4	4	71	
England	**T93**	Rd 2	4	4	4	4	4	6	4	3	5	4	4	5	3	4	5	3	6	4	76	+5 **147**
Oliver Wilson	T110	Rd 1	4	4	5	4	3	5	4	4	4	4	4	4	6	4	4	5	4	3	75	
England	**T93**	Rd 2	4	5	4	5	4	5	4	3	5	4	3	4	3	4	4	3	4	4	72	+5 **147**
Shane Lowry	T90	Rd 1	4	5	4	4	5	5	3	3	4	6	4	4	3	5	4	3	4	4	74	
Republic of Ireland	**T93**	Rd 2	4	5	4	3	4	5	4	3	5	4	3	5	3	4	4	4	5	4	73	+5 **147**

HOLE			1	2	3	4	5	6	7	8	9	10	11	12	13	14	15	16	17	18			
PAR	POS		4	4	4	4	4	5	4	3	4	4	4	4	3	5	4	3	4	4			TOTAL
Brian Harman	T32	Rd 1	4	4	4	4	5	4	4	4	3	4	4	4	2	4	5	3	5	4	71		
USA	**T93**	Rd 2	4	4	4	4	4	5	5	3	5	5	4	4	4	4	5	2	5	5	76	+5	**147**
Chesson Hadley	T72	Rd 1	4	4	3	3	4	5	3	3	4	4	5	5	3	5	4	4	5	5	73		
USA	**T93**	Rd 2	4	4	4	4	4	5	4	3	4	4	4	6	3	4	5	3	5	4	74	+5	**147**
Jon Rahm	T8	Rd 1	4	4	3	5	3	4	4	3	4	5	4	4	3	4	4	3	4	4	69		
Spain	**T93**	Rd 2	3	5	3	4	4	5	7	4	6	4	4	5	3	5	4	5	4	3	78	+5	**147**
Alex Levy	T72	Rd 1	3	6	4	5	5	4	4	2	4	4	4	4	3	5	4	4	4	4	73		
France	**T104**	Rd 2	5	4	4	4	4	6	4	4	4	3	4	4	3	5	4	5	5	3	75	+6	**148**
Dustin Johnson	T129	Rd 1	4	4	4	4	4	5	4	4	4	4	4	5	3	4	4	4	4	7	76		
USA	**T104**	Rd 2	4	4	3	4	5	5	5	3	4	4	3	5	2	4	4	2	5	6	72	+6	**148**
Bubba Watson	T110	Rd 1	3	4	5	5	5	4	4	3	5	4	4	5	3	6	4	3	4	4	75		
USA	**T104**	Rd 2	4	4	4	4	4	5	4	3	4	5	5	4	2	4	4	4	5	4	73	+6	**148**
Bronson Burgoon	T90	Rd 1	5	4	4	3	4	4	4	4	4	4	6	5	3	4	4	3	5	4	74		
USA	**T104**	Rd 2	4	4	4	5	4	4	5	3	5	4	4	3	4	4	3	5	5	4	74	+6	**148**
Nicolai Højgaard [a]	T50	Rd 1	4	5	4	3	4	5	4	3	3	4	4	5	3	5	4	3	4	5	72		
Denmark	**T104**	Rd 2	4	4	5	5	4	6	4	3	4	4	4	4	4	4	4	4	4	5	76	+6	**148**
Charles Howell III	T110	Rd 1	4	5	4	4	4	4	4	4	4	4	4	5	3	5	5	3	4	5	75		
USA	**T109**	Rd 2	4	4	4	3	4	5	4	4	4	5	4	4	3	5	5	3	5	4	74	+7	**149**
Russell Henley	T8	Rd 1	4	4	4	4	4	4	4	2	4	4	4	4	3	5	4	4	4	3	69		
USA	**T109**	Rd 2	4	5	4	4	4	6	6	4	4	4	5	5	3	5	5	3	5	4	80	+7	**149**
Ryuko Tokimatsu	T50	Rd 1	4	4	4	3	5	4	4	3	5	4	4	5	3	4	4	4	4	4	72		
Japan	**T109**	Rd 2	4	4	3	4	4	5	5	2	4	6	4	4	4	5	3	5	6		77	+7	**149**
Abraham Ancer	T32	Rd 1	4	4	4	4	4	4	4	3	5	4	4	4	3	4	4	3	4	5	71		
Mexico	**T109**	Rd 2	5	4	4	4	4	6	5	3	4	4	4	6	3	5	4	3	5	5	78	+7	**149**
Mark Calcavecchia	T72	Rd 1	4	4	4	4	4	5	4	3	5	4	4	5	3	4	4	4	4	4	73		
USA	**T109**	Rd 2	5	4	4	4	5	5	4	3	4	4	4	3	5	4	3	5	6		76	+7	**149**
Ernie Els	T72	Rd 1	5	4	4	4	4	5	4	3	4	4	4	4	3	5	4	4	4	4	73		
South Africa	**T109**	Rd 2	5	4	4	4	3	6	5	3	4	6	3	4	5	4	4	4	4		76	+7	**149**
Scott Jamieson	T110	Rd 1	4	5	5	3	4	6	4	4	4	4	4	5	3	4	4	4	4	4	75		
Scotland	**T109**	Rd 2	4	4	3	3	6	9	3	3	5	5	3	5	3	5	4	2	4	3	74	+7	**149**
Sang Hyun Park	T129	Rd 1	4	4	4	4	5	4	5	3	4	4	5	4	3	4	5	3	4	7	76		
Korea	**T109**	Rd 2	4	5	4	4	4	5	5	4	4	5	3	4	3	3	4	3	4	5	73	+7	**149**
Marcus Armitage	T149	Rd 1	5	4	4	4	4	5	4	3	5	4	5	5	3	6	5	5	5	4	80		
England	**T109**	Rd 2	4	3	3	6	4	6	4	2	4	4	3	5	3	5	3	3	4	3	69	+7	**149**
Jimmy Walker	T50	Rd 1	4	5	4	4	4	4	4	3	4	4	4	4	2	4	4	4	5	5	72		
USA	**T118**	Rd 2	4	3	5	5	4	7	4	3	4	5	4	6	3	4	4	4	4	5	78	+8	**150**
Dylan Frittelli	T32	Rd 1	4	5	4	4	5	3	4	3	5	4	3	4	4	4	3	4	4	4	71		
South Africa	**T118**	Rd 2	4	4	5	5	4	5	4	4	5	4	4	5	4	5	5	4	4	4	79	+8	**150**
Jason Kokrak	T50	Rd 1	3	4	4	3	5	5	3	4	4	4	4	4	4	4	4	4	4	4	72		
USA	**T118**	Rd 2	4	5	5	3	4	5	6	3	5	5	4	4	3	5	4	4	4	5	78	+8	**150**
Padraig Harrington	T129	Rd 1	4	4	3	4	5	5	4	2	5	5	4	5	3	5	4	4	4	6	76		
Republic of Ireland	**T118**	Rd 2	4	4	4	4	4	4	4	3	5	5	4	4	3	4	6	3	5	4	74	+8	**150**
Jazz Janewattananond	T90	Rd 1	5	4	4	3	4	4	5	3	5	6	3	5	3	4	4	3	5	4	74		
Thailand	**T118**	Rd 2	5	5	3	4	4	6	4	3	5	5	3	5	3	5	5	3	4	4	76	+8	**150**
Thomas Curtis	T154	Rd 1	4	5	4	5	4	4	4	3	5	6	5	4	4	5	4	4	6	6	82		
England	**T118**	Rd 2	4	4	3	4	4	6	4	3	3	3	4	5	3	4	4	2	4	4	68	+8	**150**

HOLE			1	2	3	4	5	6	7	8	9	10	11	12	13	14	15	16	17	18	
PAR	POS		4	4	4	4	5	4	3	4	4	4	4	3	5	4	3	4	4	4	TOTAL
Emiliano Grillo	T129	Rd 1	4	3	4	5	5	5	4	3	3	5	5	6	3	5	4	4	4	4	76
Argentina	**T118**	Rd 2	4	5	4	4	3	7	4	3	5	4	4	5	4	3	4	3	4	4	74 +8 **150**
Hideto Tanihara	T110	Rd 1	4	4	5	5	4	5	4	4	4	4	4	5	3	5	4	3	4	4	75
Japan	**T118**	Rd 2	4	4	4	3	4	6	4	4	4	5	4	4	4	5	5	3	4	4	75 +8 **150**
Anirban Lahiri	T129	Rd 1	4	4	4	5	4	5	4	3	5	6	4	4	3	5	4	4	4	4	76
India	**T118**	Rd 2	4	5	4	4	4	5	4	3	4	4	4	5	4	4	4	3	5	4	74 +8 **150**
Jhonattan Vegas	T129	Rd 1	4	5	5	4	4	4	4	3	5	4	5	4	3	5	5	3	4	5	76
Venezuela	**T118**	Rd 2	5	5	4	4	4	6	4	3	3	5	4	4	3	4	4	4	4	4	74 +8 **150**
Alexander Björk	T50	Rd 1	3	3	4	5	4	6	4	3	5	3	4	4	4	4	4	3	4	5	72
Sweden	**T118**	Rd 2	4	5	4	4	5	4	5	4	3	4	5	4	4	4	4	4	5	7	78 +8 **150**
Haraldur Magnus	T50	Rd 1	4	5	4	4	5	5	4	4	5	3	4	4	2	4	5	4	3	3	72
Iceland	**T118**	Rd 2	4	4	4	4	7	7	4	3	3	4	4	5	2	4	5	5	4	5	78 +8 **150**
Kodai Ichihara	T141	Rd 1	4	5	5	3	4	5	5	3	4	5	4	6	3	5	5	4	4	4	78
Japan	**T118**	Rd 2	4	5	3	4	3	7	4	3	4	4	4	4	3	4	4	3	5	4	72 +8 **150**
Patton Kizzire	T137	Rd 1	5	5	4	5	4	5	4	3	5	4	5	3	5	4	3	5	4	4	77
USA	**T131**	Rd 2	4	5	4	4	4	4	4	3	4	4	3	5	3	4	4	3	5	7	74 +9 **151**
Michael Hendry	T72	Rd 1	5	5	4	3	4	6	4	3	3	4	3	5	3	4	4	4	4	5	73
New Zealand	**T131**	Rd 2	4	5	4	5	4	6	4	5	4	3	4	7	3	4	4	3	5	4	78 +9 **151**
Shota Akiyoshi	T137	Rd 1	4	6	4	4	4	4	4	2	5	4	4	5	3	6	4	4	6	4	77
Japan	**T131**	Rd 2	5	3	5	4	5	5	4	3	7	4	3	5	3	4	4	3	4	3	74 +9 **151**
Todd Hamilton	T110	Rd 1	4	4	4	4	6	4	3	4	4	5	4	5	3	5	5	4	5	3	75
USA	**T131**	Rd 2	4	4	4	4	7	4	4	3	4	4	4	5	3	5	4	5	5	4	76 +9 **151**
Ryan Armour	T110	Rd 1	5	4	4	4	4	6	5	3	4	4	4	3	4	4	4	4	5	4	75
USA	**T131**	Rd 2	4	5	4	3	5	7	6	3	4	4	4	5	3	4	4	3	5	3	76 +9 **151**
Matt Jones	T110	Rd 1	5	4	4	5	4	5	4	3	4	4	4	3	5	4	3	5	6	4	75
Australia	**T131**	Rd 2	4	6	4	3	4	5	4	4	4	4	4	5	4	4	3	5	5	4	76 +9 **151**
Sandy Lyle	T110	Rd 1	4	4	4	3	5	4	4	3	4	4	5	4	5	5	4	3	5	5	75
Scotland	**T131**	Rd 2	5	5	4	4	5	5	4	4	5	4	4	5	3	4	5	3	4	3	76 +9 **151**
Retief Goosen	T90	Rd 1	4	6	4	4	4	4	4	3	5	4	5	3	4	3	6	4	4	4	74
South Africa	**T131**	Rd 2	5	4	3	4	4	7	4	3	4	5	4	6	3	3	4	5	4	5	77 +9 **151**
Danthai Boonma	T141	Rd 1	5	4	4	4	4	4	3	5	4	5	4	2	5	5	6	5	4	5	78
Thailand	**139**	Rd 2	4	5	4	3	4	7	3	3	4	3	4	4	4	4	4	6	4	4	74 +10 **152**
Jonas Blixt	T137	Rd 1	4	5	4	4	4	8	5	4	4	4	4	5	3	4	4	3	4	4	77
Sweden	**T140**	Rd 2	4	5	4	4	4	5	5	3	4	4	4	5	4	6	4	4	3	4	76 +11 **153**
Nicolas Colsaerts	T144	Rd 1	4	6	4	4	4	6	4	3	5	4	4	4	2	5	4	3	5	8	79
Belgium	**T140**	Rd 2	4	5	4	4	4	5	4	3	5	5	4	5	2	5	4	3	4	4	74 +11 **153**
Grant Forrest	T149	Rd 1	5	4	4	5	5	5	5	3	5	5	4	5	5	3	5	3	5	4	80
Scotland	**T140**	Rd 2	6	4	4	4	5	6	3	3	4	4	3	5	2	4	4	3	4	5	73 +11 **153**
Min Chel Choi	T144	Rd 1	4	5	4	4	5	6	5	4	5	4	5	4	3	5	4	4	4	4	79
Korea	**T140**	Rd 2	4	6	4	4	4	5	4	3	4	4	4	5	3	5	4	3	4	4	74 +11 **153**
Brandt Snedeker	T129	Rd 1	4	3	5	4	4	5	4	5	4	4	6	5	2	5	4	4	4	4	76
USA	**T144**	Rd 2	5	4	4	4	6	4	3	5	4	4	5	4	3	5	5	4	4	5	78 +12 **154**
Ian Poulter	T72	Rd 1	4	4	4	4	4	4	5	3	4	4	5	4	3	5	4	3	5	4	73
England	**T144**	Rd 2	4	4	4	5	3	5	7	3	4	5	5	6	2	5	5	4	4	6	81 +12 **154**
Masanori Kobayashi	T154	Rd 1	4	4	5	5	4	6	4	4	6	4	4	5	3	5	5	3	6	5	82
Japan	**T144**	Rd 2	4	4	4	3	4	4	5	3	4	5	4	4	3	4	4	4	5	4	72 +12 **154**

HOLE			1	2	3	4	5	6	7	8	9	10	11	12	13	14	15	16	17	18	
PAR	POS		4	4	4	4	4	5	4	3	4	4	4	4	3	5	4	3	4	4	TOTAL
Brady Schnell	T144	Rd 1	4	4	4	4	4	5	5	4	4	5	4	5	3	6	5	4	5	4	79
USA	**T144**	Rd 2	5	4	3	4	4	6	4	3	5	4	3	4	4	4	5	4	5	4	75 +12 **154**
Yuxin Lin [a]	T149	Rd 1	4	5	4	4	6	5	4	4	5	4	5	5	2	4	3	4	5	7	80
China	**T144**	Rd 2	3	4	4	5	4	5	4	3	4	6	3	6	3	5	4	3	4	4	74 +12 **154**
Jack Senior	T144	Rd 1	4	5	4	4	4	5	4	4	4	7	5	6	3	5	3	3	5	4	79
England	**T149**	Rd 2	5	5	4	4	3	7	4	3	3	4	5	4	4	4	4	5	4	4	76 +13 **155**
Ash Turner	T141	Rd 1	4	5	5	4	4	5	5	3	5	5	4	4	3	6	4	3	5	4	78
England	**T149**	Rd 2	4	5	4	5	4	6	4	3	5	5	4	5	2	5	5	3	4	4	77 +13 **155**
James Robinson	T110	Rd 1	4	4	5	4	4	5	5	2	4	4	4	5	4	4	4	4	4	5	75
England	**151**	Rd 2	5	4	4	4	4	5	8	4	5	4	4	4	4	4	4	4	4	6	81 +14 **156**
Andrew Landry	T149	Rd 1	4	4	4	5	4	5	5	3	4	4	4	7	3	5	4	5	4	6	80
USA	**152**	Rd 2	5	4	4	4	4	5	5	4	4	5	4	3	2	7	4	3	5	5	77 +15 **157**
Jovan Rebula [a]	T144	Rd 1	5	5	4	4	4	5	4	3	6	4	4	5	3	6	5	3	6	3	79
South Africa	**T153**	Rd 2	4	5	4	4	5	5	5	3	5	4	5	5	2	4	6	4	4	5	79 +16 **158**
Jens Dantorp	T129	Rd 1	3	4	4	6	4	5	5	5	4	4	4	4	3	3	5	2	6	5	76
Sweden	**T153**	Rd 2	4	4	4	4	5	5	6	4	5	4	5	6	3	6	5	3	4	5	82 +16 **158**
Darren Clarke	T154	Rd 1	4	6	5	5	4	4	4	3	4	6	5	5	3	4	5	4	4	6	82
Northern Ireland	**155**	Rd 2	5	5	5	4	5	7	4	4	3	5	4	6	3	4	4	4	5	6	83 +23 **165**
David Duval	T149	Rd 1	5	4	4	4	7	7	3	4	4	3	5	3	3	4	6	3	5	6	80 WD
USA																					

THE TOP TENS

Driving Distance

1 Lucas Herbert 331.0
2 Gavin Green 330.0
3 Xander Schauffele 327.0
4 Brendan Steele 325.8
5 Rory McIlroy 323.9
6 Luke List 322.5
7 Bryson DeChambeau .. 321.9
8 Ryan Fox 320.3
9 Kevin Chappell 319.5
9 Rickie Fowler 319.5
37 *Francesco Molinari 307.4*

Fairways Hit

Maximum of 60

1 Erik van Rooyen 42
1 Marcus Kinhult 42
3 Bernhard Langer 41
3 Paul Casey 41
5 Tiger Woods 40
5 Webb Simpson 40
5 Shubhankar Sharma 40
8 Eddie Pepperell 39
8 Stewart Cink 39
8 Rickie Fowler 39
8 Brendan Steele 39
74 *Francesco Molinari 26*

Greens in Regulation

Maximum of 72

1 Tommy Fleetwood 55
2 Tony Finau 54
3 Phil Mickelson 53
3 Louis Oosthuizen 53
3 Brendan Steele 53
6 Danny Willett 52
6 Kyle Stanley 52
8 Patrick Cantlay 51
9 Thorbjørn Olesen 50
9 Webb Simpson 50
9 Erik van Rooyen 50
9 Charley Hoffman 50
9 Austin Cook 50
9 Tyrrell Hatton 50
9 Jason Dufner 50
23 *Francesco Molinari 48*

Putts

1 Kevin Kisner 107
2 Julian Suri 108
3 Xander Schauffele 110
4 *Francesco Molinari 111*
4 Patrick Reed 111
4 Rickie Fowler 111
7 Justin Rose 113
7 Matt Kuchar 113
7 Pat Perez 113
7 Michael Kim 113
7 Paul Dunne 113

Statistical Rankings

	Driving Distance	Rank	Fairways Hit	Rank	Greens In Regulation	Rank	Putts	Rank
Byeong Hun An	303.0	51	33	40	47	30	122	51
Kiradech Aphibarnrat	299.4	62	28	65	38	76	119	39
Keegan Bradley	310.6	25	34	31	43	59	125	67
Rafa Cabrera Bello	306.0	43	36	18	46	40	124	62
Patrick Cantlay	311.8	24	27	70	51	8	121	45
Paul Casey	313.5	18	41	3	47	30	123	58
Kevin Chappell	319.5	9	33	40	47	30	115	15
Stewart Cink	313.4	20	39	8	47	30	119	39
Austin Cook	301.8	58	34	31	50	9	122	51
Sean Crocker	313.6	17	31	50	44	53	118	32
Cameron Davis	302.4	53	37	16	48	23	118	32
Jason Day	306.4	41	28	65	42	64	114	12
Bryson DeChambeau	321.9	7	25	76	39	71	117	24
Jason Dufner	310.4	27	35	25	50	9	125	67
Paul Dunne	306.6	40	28	65	35	79	113	7
Rhys Enoch	295.3	68	32	47	44	53	121	45
Tony Finau	315.0	15	35	25	54	2	126	70
Ross Fisher	309.6	30	37	16	47	30	122	51
Tommy Fleetwood	318.4	11	32	47	55	1	123	58
Rickie Fowler	319.5	9	39	8	42	64	111	4
Ryan Fox	320.3	8	26	74	46	40	117	24
Gavin Green	330.0	2	36	18	45	49	122	51
Adam Hadwin	290.5	73	34	31	44	53	118	32
Tyrrell Hatton	308.3	34	35	25	50	9	126	70
Lucas Herbert	331.0	1	36	18	45	49	122	51
Charley Hoffman	304.1	48	28	65	65	50	119	39
Beau Hossler	300.0	61	23	79	46	40	127	75
Yuta Ikeda	299.4	62	38	12	47	30	124	62
Zach Johnson	291.6	72	29	59	45	49	117	24
Sung Kang	284.1	78	28	65	39	71	118	32
Masahiro Kawamura	301.5	60	34	31	47	30	122	51
Michael Kim	304.1	48	36	18	39	71	113	7
Si Woo Kim	301.6	59	36	18	47	30	124	62
Marcus Kinhult	308.3	34	42	1	49	16	124	62
Kevin Kisner	309.3	31	29	59	43	59	107	1
Satoshi Kodaira	298.9	64	33	40	42	64	117	24
Brooks Koepka	310.6	25	29	59	44	53	117	24
Matt Kuchar	288.0	75	35	25	43	59	113	7
Bernhard Langer	265.5	79	41	3	49	16	125	67
Marc Leishman	286.4	77	33	40	43	59	116	21

	Driving Distance	Rank	Fairways Hit	Rank	Greens In Regulation	Rank	Putts	Rank
Tom Lewis	307.4	37	31	50	48	23	123	58
Haotong Li	313.5	18	34	31	46	40	121	45
Luke List	322.5	6	31	50	47	30	122	51
Sam Locke [a]	306.4	41	34	31	38	76	116	21
Zander Lombard	304.6	46	24	78	46	40	123	58
Rory McIlroy	323.9	5	27	70	49	16	114	12
Phil Mickelson	302.3	56	31	50	53	3	120	42
Yusaku Miyazato	308.8	32	38	12	49	16	120	42
Francesco Molinari	307.4	37	26	74	48	23	111	4
Ryan Moore	302.0	57	33	40	45	49	114	12
Kevin Na	294.0	70	33	40	41	68	118	32
Alex Noren	305.0	45	31	50	47	30	118	32
Shaun Norris	298.8	65	30	56	39	71	115	15
Thorbjørn Olesen	317.6	12	36	18	50	9	120	42
Louis Oosthuizen	312.5	21	38	12	53	3	129	76
Eddie Pepperell	289.0	74	39	8	49	16	117	24
Pat Perez	286.8	76	35	25	46	40	113	7
Thomas Pieters	307.9	36	25	76	46	40	117	24
Patrick Reed	308.8	32	27	70	39	71	111	4
Justin Rose	310.0	29	36	18	49	16	113	7
Brett Rumford	294.5	69	29	59	41	68	116	21
Xander Schauffele	327.0	3	38	12	43	59	110	3
Adam Scott	306.8	39	32	47	48	23	117	24
Shubhankar Sharma	296.1	67	40	5	41	68	115	15
Webb Simpson	314.4	16	40	5	50	9	121	45
Cameron Smith	305.1	44	33	40	38	76	115	15
Matthew Southgate	310.3	28	29	59	44	53	124	62
Jordan Spieth	312.1	23	30	56	46	40	115	15
Kyle Stanley	302.4	53	27	70	52	6	129	76
Brendan Steele	325.8	4	39	8	53	3	129	76
Henrik Stenson	298.8	65	35	25	48	23	121	45
Brandon Stone	316.5	13	29	59	49	16	126	70
Julian Suri	302.4	53	31	50	42	64	108	2
Erik van Rooyen	315.5	14	42	1	50	9	121	45
Lee Westwood	304.5	47	34	31	46	40	126	70
Danny Willett	312.3	22	30	56	52	6	126	70
Chris Wood	292.8	71	34	31	44	53	115	15
Gary Woodland	303.5	50	34	31	48	23	129	76
Tiger Woods	303.0	51	40	5	48	23	118	32

	Driving Distance	Rank	Fairways Hit	Rank	Greens In Regulation	Rank	Putts	Rank
Shota Akiyoshi	296.3	103	15	83	18	133	60	55
Abraham Ancer	293.3	115	15	83	26	16	68	152
Marcus Armitage	278.8	143	6	155	16	147	55	6
Ryan Armour	294.0	112	15	83	17	145	61	76
Daniel Berger	327.0	10	18	36	19	113	62	97
Alexander Björk	268.8	152	17	49	20	100	60	55
Jonas Blixt	294.3	111	18	36	22	59	62	97
Danthai Boonma	301.5	91	16	68	19	113	61	76
Bronson Burgoon	300.8	98	16	68	20	100	62	97
Mark Calcavecchia	292.0	120	20	12	21	83	64	122
Jorge Campillo	287.5	127	17	49	18	133	60	55
Min Chel Choi	311.3	57	14	100	15	153	62	97
Darren Clarke	284.5	131	13	117	12	154	65	135
George Coetzee	305.5	76	10	149	20	100	57	16
Nicolas Colsaerts	321.5	20	12	134	21	83	59	45
Thomas Curtis	278.5	144	12	134	22	59	60	55
Jens Dantorp	319.3	24	12	134	17	145	62	97
Ernie Els	304.8	80	10	149	19	113	61	76
Matthew Fitzpatrick	293.0	116	17	49	21	83	63	113
Grant Forrest	308.3	64	14	100	16	147	59	45
Dylan Frittelli	322.5	17	17	49	23	47	68	152
Sergio Garcia	328.8	8	16	68	21	83	60	55
Retief Goosen	280.8	138	12	134	22	59	65	135
Branden Grace	295.0	109	18	36	22	59	62	97
Emiliano Grillo	313.0	50	19	22	20	100	65	135
Chesson Hadley	282.8	134	14	100	19	113	60	55
Todd Hamilton	256.8	155	21	6	19	113	63	113
Brian Harman	307.8	65	16	68	21	83	61	76
Padraig Harrington	296.5	102	13	117	18	133	59	45
Michael Hendry	271.0	150	18	36	19	113	59	45
Russell Henley	312.8	51	18	36	23	47	65	135
Nicolai Højgaard [a]	331.8	4	13	117	20	100	61	76
Charles Howell III	286.5	128	20	12	22	59	66	147
Kodai Ichihara	294.0	112	14	100	18	133	57	16
Scott Jamieson	303.8	87	13	117	21	83	57	16
Jazz Janewattananond	273.3	149	18	36	18	133	60	55
Dustin Johnson	341.8	1	15	83	21	83	60	55
Matt Jones	295.3	108	13	117	19	113	64	122
Martin Kaymer	313.5	47	17	49	19	113	60	55
Patton Kizzire	324.3	13	19	22	22	59	66	147
Russell Knox	302.8	88	15	83	18	133	58	30
Masanori Kobayashi	305.3	78	12	134	20	100	66	147
Jason Kokrak	319.3	24	17	49	22	59	62	97
Kelly Kraft	285.3	129	19	22	16	147	55	6
Anirban Lahiri	278.3	145	12	134	21	83	64	122
Andrew Landry	301.0	95	15	83	19	113	65	135
Tom Lehman	296.0	105	19	22	19	113	57	16
Alex Levy	310.3	60	15	83	22	59	62	97
Yuxin Lin [a]	301.3	92	13	117	21	83	65	135
Shane Lowry	309.5	62	15	83	20	100	60	55
Sandy Lyle	282.0	136	17	49	12	154	55	6
Haraldur Magnus	304.3	83	19	22	18	133	57	16
Hideki Matsuyama	323.3	14	15	83	22	59	62	97
Sang Hyun Park	312.0	54	15	83	21	83	64	122
Ian Poulter	313.5	47	14	100	19	113	60	55
Jon Rahm	319.3	24	14	100	25	24	64	122
Chez Reavie	301.0	95	23	1	20	100	61	76
Jovan Rebula [a]	279.8	139	10	149	16	147	64	122
James Robinson	315.5	42	14	100	22	59	68	152
Brady Schnell	274.8	148	13	117	16	147	63	113
Charl Schwartzel	321.5	20	15	83	19	113	56	13
Jack Senior	289.5	124	16	68	16	147	61	76
Jordan Smith	285.0	130	13	117	18	133	61	76
Brandt Snedeker	292.8	118	9	153	18	133	61	76
Andy Sullivan	302.0	89	18	36	23	47	62	97
Hideto Tanihara	301.0	95	22	2	24	35	69	155
Justin Thomas	323.0	16	18	36	23	47	60	55
Ryuko Tokimatsu	284.0	132	19	22	18	133	59	45
Ash Turner	287.8	125	8	154	18	133	64	122
Peter Uihlein	293.5	114	14	100	23	47	61	76
Jhonattan Vegas	315.8	40	12	134	20	100	63	113
Jimmy Walker	306.0	74	15	83	19	113	61	76
Matt Wallace	295.8	107	20	12	22	59	60	55
Bubba Watson	320.0	23	13	117	24	35	67	151
Oliver Wilson	281.5	137	13	117	24	35	65	135
Fabrizio Zanotti	279.8	139	20	12	24	35	62	97

Roll of Honour

Year	Champion	Score	Margin	Runners-up	Venue
1860	Willie Park Sr	174	2	Tom Morris Sr	Prestwick
1861	Tom Morris Sr	163	4	Willie Park Sr	Prestwick
1862	Tom Morris Sr	163	13	Willie Park Sr	Prestwick
1863	Willie Park Sr	168	2	Tom Morris Sr	Prestwick
1864	Tom Morris Sr	167	2	Andrew Strath	Prestwick
1865	Andrew Strath	162	2	Willie Park Sr	Prestwick
1866	Willie Park Sr	169	2	David Park	Prestwick
1867	Tom Morris Sr	170	2	Willie Park Sr	Prestwick
1868	Tommy Morris Jr	154	3	Tom Morris Sr	Prestwick
1869	Tommy Morris Jr	157	11	Bob Kirk	Prestwick
1870	Tommy Morris Jr	149	12	Bob Kirk, Davie Strath	Prestwick
1871	*No Championship*				
1872	Tommy Morris Jr	166	3	Davie Strath	Prestwick
1873	Tom Kidd	179	1	Jamie Anderson	St Andrews
1874	Mungo Park	159	2	Tommy Morris Jr	Musselburgh
1875	Willie Park Sr	166	2	Bob Martin	Prestwick
1876	Bob Martin	176	—	Davie Strath	St Andrews
	(Martin was awarded the title when Strath refused to play-off)				
1877	Jamie Anderson	160	2	Bob Pringle	Musselburgh
1878	Jamie Anderson	157	2	Bob Kirk	Prestwick
1879	Jamie Anderson	169	3	Jamie Allan, Andrew Kirkaldy	St Andrews
1880	Bob Ferguson	162	5	Peter Paxton	Musselburgh
1881	Bob Ferguson	170	3	Jamie Anderson	Prestwick
1882	Bob Ferguson	171	3	Willie Fernie	St Andrews
1883	Willie Fernie	158	Play-off	Bob Ferguson	Musselburgh
1884	Jack Simpson	160	4	Douglas Rolland, Willie Fernie	Prestwick
1885	Bob Martin	171	1	Archie Simpson	St Andrews
1886	David Brown	157	2	Willie Campbell	Musselburgh
1887	Willie Park Jr	161	1	Bob Martin	Prestwick
1888	Jack Burns	171	1	David Anderson Jr, Ben Sayers	St Andrews
1889	Willie Park Jr	155	Play-off	Andrew Kirkaldy	Musselburgh
1890	John Ball Jr[a]	164	3	Willie Fernie, Archie Simpson	Prestwick
1891	Hugh Kirkaldy	166	2	Willie Fernie, Andrew Kirkaldy	St Andrews
	(From 1892 the Championship was extended to 72 holes)				
1892	Harold Hilton[a]	305	3	John Ball Jr[a], Hugh Kirkaldy, Sandy Herd	Muirfield
1893	Willie Auchterlonie	322	2	John Laidlay[a]	Prestwick

Tommy Armour, 1931   *Ben Hogan, 1953*   *Gary Player, 1968*

Year	Champion	Score	Margin	Runners-up	Venue
1894	JH Taylor	326	5	Douglas Rolland	St George's
1895	JH Taylor	322	4	Sandy Herd	St Andrews
1896	Harry Vardon	316	Play-off	JH Taylor	Muirfield
1897	Harold Hilton[a]	314	1	James Braid	Royal Liverpool
1898	Harry Vardon	307	1	Willie Park Jr	Prestwick
1899	Harry Vardon	310	5	Jack White	St George's
1900	JH Taylor	309	8	Harry Vardon	St Andrews
1901	James Braid	309	3	Harry Vardon	Muirfield
1902	Sandy Herd	307	1	Harry Vardon, James Braid	Royal Liverpool
1903	Harry Vardon	300	6	Tom Vardon	Prestwick
1904	Jack White	296	1	James Braid, JH Taylor	Royal St George's
1905	James Braid	318	5	JH Taylor, Rowland Jones	St Andrews
1906	James Braid	300	4	JH Taylor	Muirfield
1907	Arnaud Massy	312	2	JH Taylor	Royal Liverpool
1908	James Braid	291	8	Tom Ball	Prestwick
1909	JH Taylor	295	6	James Braid, Tom Ball	Cinque Ports
1910	James Braid	299	4	Sandy Herd	St Andrews
1911	Harry Vardon	303	Play-off	Arnaud Massy	Royal St George's
1912	Ted Ray	295	4	Harry Vardon	Muirfield
1913	JH Taylor	304	8	Ted Ray	Royal Liverpool
1914	Harry Vardon	306	3	JH Taylor	Prestwick

1915-1919 No Championship

Year	Champion	Score	Margin	Runners-up	Venue
1920	George Duncan	303	2	Sandy Herd	Royal Cinque Ports
1921	Jock Hutchison	296	Play-off	Roger Wethered[a]	St Andrews
1922	Walter Hagen	300	1	George Duncan, Jim Barnes	Royal St George's
1923	Arthur Havers	295	1	Walter Hagen	Troon
1924	Walter Hagen	301	1	Ernest Whitcombe	Royal Liverpool
1925	Jim Barnes	300	1	Archie Compston, Ted Ray	Prestwick
1926	Bobby Jones[a]	291	2	Al Watrous	Royal Lytham
1927	Bobby Jones[a]	285	6	Aubrey Boomer, Fred Robson	St Andrews
1928	Walter Hagen	292	2	Gene Sarazen	Royal St George's
1929	Walter Hagen	292	6	Johnny Farrell	Muirfield
1930	Bobby Jones[a]	291	2	Leo Diegel, Macdonald Smith	Royal Liverpool
1931	Tommy Armour	296	1	Jose Jurado	Carnoustie

Year	Champion	Score	Margin	Runners-up	Venue
1932	Gene Sarazen	283	5	Macdonald Smith	Prince's
1933	Denny Shute	292	Play-off	Craig Wood	St Andrews
1934	Henry Cotton	283	5	Sid Brews	Royal St George's
1935	Alf Perry	283	4	Alf Padgham	Muirfield
1936	Alf Padgham	287	1	Jimmy Adams	Royal Liverpool
1937	Henry Cotton	290	2	Reg Whitcombe	Carnoustie
1938	Reg Whitcombe	295	2	Jimmy Adams	Royal St George's
1939	Dick Burton	290	2	Johnny Bulla	St Andrews
1940-1945 No Championship					
1946	Sam Snead	290	4	Bobby Locke, Johnny Bulla	St Andrews
1947	Fred Daly	293	1	Reg Horne, Frank Stranahan[a]	Royal Liverpool
1948	Henry Cotton	284	5	Fred Daly	Muirfield
1949	Bobby Locke	283	Play-off	Harry Bradshaw	Royal St George's
1950	Bobby Locke	279	2	Roberto de Vicenzo	Troon
1951	Max Faulkner	285	2	Antonio Cerda	Royal Portrush
1952	Bobby Locke	287	1	Peter Thomson	Royal Lytham
1953	Ben Hogan	282	4	Frank Stranahan[a], Dai Rees, Peter Thomson, Antonio Cerda	Carnoustie
1954	Peter Thomson	283	1	Syd Scott, Dai Rees, Bobby Locke	Royal Birkdale
1955	Peter Thomson	281	2	John Fallon	St Andrews
1956	Peter Thomson	286	3	Flory Van Donck	Royal Liverpool
1957	Bobby Locke	279	3	Peter Thomson	St Andrews
1958	Peter Thomson	278	Play-off	Dave Thomas	Royal Lytham
1959	Gary Player	284	2	Flory Van Donck, Fred Bullock	Muirfield
1960	Kel Nagle	278	1	Arnold Palmer	St Andrews
1961	Arnold Palmer	284	1	Dai Rees	Royal Birkdale
1962	Arnold Palmer	276	6	Kel Nagle	Troon

(Prior to 1963, scores assessed against "level 4s". From 1963, pars were introduced and holes were played in 3, 4 or 5 shots.)

Year	Champion	To Par	Score	Margin	Runners-up	Venue
1963	Bob Charles	-3	277	Play-off	Phil Rodgers	Royal Lytham
1964	Tony Lema	-9	279	5	Jack Nicklaus	St Andrews
1965	Peter Thomson	-7	285	2	Christy O'Connor Sr, Brian Huggett	Royal Birkdale
1966	Jack Nicklaus	-2	282	1	Dave Thomas, Doug Sanders	Muirfield
1967	Roberto de Vicenzo	-10	278	2	Jack Nicklaus	Royal Liverpool
1968	Gary Player	+1	289	2	Jack Nicklaus, Bob Charles	Carnoustie
1969	Tony Jacklin	-4	280	2	Bob Charles	Royal Lytham
1970	Jack Nicklaus	-5	283	Play-off	Doug Sanders	St Andrews
1971	Lee Trevino	-14	278	1	Liang Huan Lu	Royal Birkdale
1972	Lee Trevino	-6	278	1	Jack Nicklaus	Muirfield
1973	Tom Weiskopf	-12	276	3	Neil Coles, Johnny Miller	Troon
1974	Gary Player	-2	282	4	Peter Oosterhuis	Royal Lytham
1975	Tom Watson	-9	279	Play-off	Jack Newton	Carnoustie
1976	Johnny Miller	-9	279	6	Jack Nicklaus, Seve Ballesteros	Royal Birkdale
1977	Tom Watson	-12	268	1	Jack Nicklaus	Turnberry
1978	Jack Nicklaus	-7	281	2	Simon Owen, Ben Crenshaw, Ray Floyd, Tom Kite	St Andrews
1979	Seve Ballesteros	-1	283	3	Jack Nicklaus, Ben Crenshaw	Royal Lytham
1980	Tom Watson	-13	271	4	Lee Trevino	Muirfield
1981	Bill Rogers	-4	276	4	Bernhard Langer	Royal St George's
1982	Tom Watson	-4	284	1	Peter Oosterhuis, Nick Price	Royal Troon
1983	Tom Watson	-9	275	1	Hale Irwin, Andy Bean	Royal Birkdale
1984	Seve Ballesteros	-12	276	2	Bernhard Langer, Tom Watson	St Andrews

Tom Watson, 1975

Paul Lawrie, 1999

Padraig Harrington, 2007

Year	Champion	To Par	Score	Margin	Runners-up	Venue
1985	Sandy Lyle	+2	282	1	Payne Stewart	Royal St George's
1986	Greg Norman	E	280	5	Gordon J Brand	Turnberry
1987	Nick Faldo	-5	279	1	Rodger Davis, Paul Azinger	Muirfield
1988	Seve Ballesteros	-11	273	2	Nick Price	Royal Lytham
1989	Mark Calcavecchia	-13	275	Play-off	Greg Norman, Wayne Grady	Royal Troon
1990	Nick Faldo	-18	270	5	Mark McNulty, Payne Stewart	St Andrews
1991	Ian Baker-Finch	-8	272	2	Mike Harwood	Royal Birkdale
1992	Nick Faldo	-12	272	1	John Cook	Muirfield
1993	Greg Norman	-13	267	2	Nick Faldo	Royal St George's
1994	Nick Price	-12	268	1	Jesper Parnevik	Turnberry
1995	John Daly	-6	282	Play-off	Costantino Rocca	St Andrews
1996	Tom Lehman	-13	271	2	Mark McCumber, Ernie Els	Royal Lytham
1997	Justin Leonard	-12	272	3	Jesper Parnevik, Darren Clarke	Royal Troon
1998	Mark O'Meara	E	280	Play-off	Brian Watts	Royal Birkdale
1999	Paul Lawrie	+6	290	Play-off	Justin Leonard, Jean van de Velde	Carnoustie
2000	Tiger Woods	-19	269	8	Ernie Els, Thomas Bjørn	St Andrews
2001	David Duval	-10	274	3	Niclas Fasth	Royal Lytham
2002	Ernie Els	-6	278	Play-off	Thomas Levet, Stuart Appleby, Steve Elkington	Muirfield
2003	Ben Curtis	-1	283	1	Thomas Bjørn, Vijay Singh	Royal St George's
2004	Todd Hamilton	-10	274	Play-off	Ernie Els	Royal Troon
2005	Tiger Woods	-14	274	5	Colin Montgomerie	St Andrews
2006	Tiger Woods	-18	270	2	Chris DiMarco	Royal Liverpool
2007	Padraig Harrington	-7	277	Play-off	Sergio Garcia	Carnoustie
2008	Padraig Harrington	+3	283	4	Ian Poulter	Royal Birkdale
2009	Stewart Cink	-2	278	Play-off	Tom Watson	Turnberry
2010	Louis Oosthuizen	-16	272	7	Lee Westwood	St Andrews
2011	Darren Clarke	-5	275	3	Phil Mickelson, Dustin Johnson	Royal St George's
2012	Ernie Els	-7	273	1	Adam Scott	Royal Lytham
2013	Phil Mickelson	-3	281	3	Henrik Stenson	Muirfield
2014	Rory McIlroy	-17	271	2	Sergio Garcia, Rickie Fowler	Royal Liverpool
2015	Zach Johnson	-15	273	Play-off	Louis Oosthuizen, Marc Leishman	St Andrews
2016	Henrik Stenson	-20	264	3	Phil Mickelson	Royal Troon
2017	Jordan Spieth	-12	268	3	Matt Kuchar	Royal Birkdale
2018	Francesco Molinari	-8	276	2	Justin Rose, Rory McIlroy, Kevin Kisner, Xander Schauffele	Carnoustie

Records

Most Victories

6: Harry Vardon, 1896, 1898, 1899, 1903, 1911, 1914
5: James Braid, 1901, 1905, 1906, 1908, 1910; JH Taylor, 1894, 1895, 1900, 1909, 1913; Peter Thomson, 1954, 1955, 1956, 1958, 1965; Tom Watson, 1975, 1977, 1980, 1982, 1983

Most Runner-Up or Joint Runner-Up Finishes

7: Jack Nicklaus, 1964, 1967, 1968, 1972, 1976, 1977, 1979
6: JH Taylor, 1896, 1904, 1905, 1906, 1907, 1914

Oldest Winners

Tom Morris Sr, 1867, 46 years 102 days
Roberto de Vicenzo, 1967, 44 years 92 days
Harry Vardon, 1914, 44 years 41 days
Tom Morris Sr, 1864, 43 years 92 days
Phil Mickelson, 2013, 43 years 35 days
Darren Clarke, 2011, 42 years 337 days
Ernie Els, 2012, 42 years 279 days

Youngest Winners

Tommy Morris Jr, 1868, 17 years 156 days
Tommy Morris Jr, 1869, 18 years 149 days
Tommy Morris Jr, 1870, 19 years 148 days
Willie Auchterlonie, 1893, 21 years 22 days
Tommy Morris Jr, 1872, 21 years 146 days
Seve Ballesteros, 1979, 22 years 103 days

Known Oldest and Youngest Competitors

74 years, 11 months, 24 days: Tom Morris Sr, 1896
74 years, 4 months, 9 days: Gene Sarazen, 1976
14 years, 4 months, 25 days: Tommy Morris Jr, 1865

Largest Margin of Victory

13 strokes, Tom Morris Sr, 1862
12 strokes, Tommy Morris Jr, 1870
11 strokes, Tommy Morris Jr, 1869
8 strokes, JH Taylor, 1900 and 1913; James Braid, 1908; Tiger Woods, 2000

Lowest Winning Total by a Champion

264, Henrik Stenson, Royal Troon, 2016 – 68, 65, 68, 63
267, Greg Norman, Royal St George's, 1993 – 66, 68, 69, 64

268, Tom Watson, Turnberry, 1977 – 68, 70, 65, 65; Nick Price, Turnberry, 1994 – 69, 66, 67, 66; Jordan Spieth, Royal Birkdale, 2017 – 65, 69, 65, 69

Lowest Total in Relation to Par Since 1963

20 under par: Henrik Stenson, 2016 (264)
19 under par: Tiger Woods, St Andrews, 2000 (269)
18 under par: Nick Faldo, St Andrews, 1990 (270); Tiger Woods, Royal Liverpool, 2006 (270)

Lowest Total by a Runner-Up

267: Phil Mickelson, Royal Troon, 2016 – 63, 69, 70, 65
269: Jack Nicklaus, Turnberry, 1977 – 68, 70, 65, 66; Nick Faldo, Royal St George's, 1993 – 69, 63, 70, 67; Jesper Parnevik, Turnberry, 1994 – 68, 66, 68, 67

Lowest Total by an Amateur

277: Jordan Niebrugge, St Andrews, 2015 – 67, 73, 67, 70

Lowest Individual Round

62: Branden Grace, third round, Royal Birkdale, 2017
63: Mark Hayes, second round, Turnberry, 1977; Isao Aoki, third round, Muirfield, 1980; Greg Norman, second round, Turnberry, 1986; Paul Broadhurst, third round, St Andrews, 1990; Jodie Mudd, fourth round, Royal Birkdale, 1991; Nick Faldo, second round, Royal St George's, 1993; Payne Stewart, fourth round, Royal St George's, 1993; Rory McIlroy, first round, St Andrews, 2010; Phil Mickelson, first round, Royal Troon, 2016; Henrik Stenson, fourth round, Royal Troon, 2016; Haotong Li, fourth round, Royal Birkdale, 2017

Lowest Individual Round by an Amateur

65: Tom Lewis, first round, Royal St George's, 2011

Lowest First Round

63: Rory McIlroy, St Andrews, 2010; Phil Mickelson, Royal Troon, 2016

Lowest Second Round

63: Mark Hayes, Turnberry, 1977; Greg Norman, Turnberry, 1986; Nick Faldo, Royal St George's, 1993

Lowest Third Round

62: Branden Grace, Royal Birkdale, 2017

Lowest Fourth Round

63: Jodie Mudd, Royal Birkdale, 1991; Payne Stewart, Royal St George's, 1993; Henrik Stenson, Royal Troon, 2016; Haotong Li, Royal Birkdale, 2017

Lowest Score over the First 36 Holes

130: Nick Faldo, Muirfield, 1992 – 66, 64; Brandt Snedeker, Royal Lytham & St Annes, 2012 – 66, 64

Lowest Score over the Middle 36 Holes

130: Fuzzy Zoeller, Turnberry, 1994 – 66, 64

Lowest Score over the Final 36 Holes

130: Tom Watson, Turnberry, 1977 – 65, 65; Ian Baker-Finch, Royal Birkdale, 1991 – 64, 66; Anders Forsbrand, Turnberry, 1994 – 66, 64; Marc Leishman, St Andrews, 2015 – 64, 66

Lowest Score over the First 54 Holes

198: Tom Lehman, Royal Lytham & St Annes, 1996 – 67, 67, 64
199: Nick Faldo, St Andrews, 1990 – 67, 65, 67; Nick Faldo, Muirfield, 1992 – 66, 64, 69; Adam Scott, Royal Lytham & St Annes, 2012 – 64, 67, 68; Jordan Spieth, Royal Birkdale, 2017 – 65, 69, 65

Lowest Score over the Final 54 Holes

196: Henrik Stenson, Royal Troon, 2016 – 65, 68, 63
199: Nick Price, Turnberry, 1994 – 66, 67, 66

Lowest Score for Nine Holes

28: Denis Durnian, first nine, Royal Birkdale, 1983
29: Tom Haliburton, first nine, Royal Lytham & St Annes, 1963; Peter Thomson, first nine, Royal Lytham & St Annes, 1963; Tony Jacklin, first nine, St Andrews, 1970; Bill Longmuir, first nine, Royal Lytham & St Annes, 1979; David J Russell first nine, Royal Lytham & St Annes, 1988; Ian Baker-Finch, first nine, St Andrews, 1990; Paul Broadhurst, first nine, St Andrews, 1990; Ian Baker-Finch, first nine, Royal Birkdale, 1991; Paul McGinley, first nine, Royal Lytham & St Annes, 1996; Ernie Els, first nine, Muirfield, 2002; Sergio Garcia, first nine, Royal Liverpool, 2006; David Lingmerth, first nine, St Andrews, 2015; Matt Kuchar, first nine, Royal Birkdale, 2017; Branden Grace, first nine, Royal Birkdale, 2017

Most Successive Victories

4: Tommy Morris Jr, 1868-72 (No Championship in 1871)
3: Jamie Anderson, 1877-79; Bob Ferguson, 1880-82; Peter Thomson, 1954-56
2: Tom Morris Sr, 1861-62; JH Taylor, 1894-95; Harry Vardon, 1898-99; James Braid, 1905-06; Bobby Jones, 1926-27; Walter Hagen, 1928-29; Bobby Locke, 1949-50; Arnold Palmer, 1961-62; Lee Trevino, 1971-72; Tom Watson, 1982-83; Tiger Woods, 2005-06; Padraig Harrington, 2007-08

Amateurs Who Have Won The Open

3: Bobby Jones, Royal Lytham & St Annes, 1926; St Andrews, 1927; Royal Liverpool, 1930
2: Harold Hilton, Muirfield, 1892; Royal Liverpool, 1897
1: John Ball Jr, Prestwick, 1890

Champions Who Won on Debut

Willie Park Sr, Prestwick, 1860; Tom Kidd, St Andrews, 1873; Mungo Park, Musselburgh, 1874; Jock Hutchison, St Andrews, 1921; Denny Shute, St Andrews, 1933; Ben Hogan, Carnoustie, 1953; Tony Lema, St Andrews, 1964; Tom Watson, Carnoustie, 1975; Ben Curtis, Royal St George's, 2003

Attendance

Year	Total
1960	39,563
1961	21,708
1962	37,098
1963	24,585
1964	35,954
1965	32,927
1966	40,182
1967	29,880
1968	51,819
1969	46,001
1970	81,593
1971	70,076
1972	84,746
1973	78,810
1974	92,796
1975	85,258
1976	92,021
1977	87,615
1978	125,271
1979	134,501
1980	131,610
1981	111,987
1982	133,299
1983	142,892
1984	193,126
1985	141,619
1986	134,261
1987	139,189
1988	191,334
1989	160,639
1990	208,680
1991	189,435
1992	146,427
1993	141,000
1994	128,000
1995	180,000
1996	170,000
1997	176,000
1998	195,100
1999	157,000
2000	239,000
2001	178,000
2002	161,500
2003	183,000
2004	176,000
2005	223,000
2006	230,000
2007	154,000
2008	201,500
2009	123,000
2010	201,000
2011	180,100
2012	181,300
2013	142,036
2014	202,917
2015	237,024
2016	173,134
2017	235,000
2018	172,000

Greatest Interval Between First and Last Victory

19 years: JH Taylor, 1894-1913
18 years: Harry Vardon, 1896-1914
15 years: Willie Park Sr, 1860-75; Gary Player, 1959-74
14 years: Henry Cotton, 1934-48

Greatest Interval Between Victories

11 years: Henry Cotton, 1937-48 (*No Championship 1940-45*)
10 years: Ernie Els, 2002-12
9 years: Willie Park Sr, 1866-75; Bob Martin, 1876-85; JH Taylor, 1900-09; Gary Player, 1959-68

Champions Who Have Won in Three Separate Decades

Harry Vardon, 1896, 1898 & 1899/1903/1911 & 1914
JH Taylor, 1894 & 1895/1900 & 1909/1913
Gary Player, 1959/1968/1974

Competitors with the Most Top Five Finishes

16: JH Taylor; Jack Nicklaus

Competitors Who Have Recorded the Most Rounds Under Par From 1963

59: Jack Nicklaus
54: Nick Faldo

Competitors with the Most Finishes Under Par From 1963

15: Ernie Els
14: Jack Nicklaus; Nick Faldo
13: Tom Watson

Champions Who Have Led Outright After Every Round

72 hole Championships
Ted Ray, 1912; Bobby Jones, 1927; Gene Sarazen, 1932; Henry Cotton, 1934; Tom Weiskopf, 1973; Tiger Woods, 2005; Rory McIlroy, 2014
36 hole Championships
Willie Park Sr, 1860 and 1866; Tom Morris Sr, 1862 and 1864; Tommy Morris Jr, 1869 and 1870; Mungo Park, 1874; Jamie Anderson, 1879; Bob Ferguson, 1880, 1881, 1882; Willie Fernie, 1883; Jack Simpson, 1884; Hugh Kirkaldy, 1891

Largest Leads Since 1892

After 18 holes:
5 strokes: Sandy Herd, 1896
4 strokes: Harry Vardon, 1902; Jim Barnes, 1925; Christy O'Connor Jr, 1985
After 36 holes:
9 strokes: Henry Cotton, 1934
6 strokes: Abe Mitchell, 1920
After 54 holes:
10 strokes: Henry Cotton, 1934
7 strokes: Harry Vardon, 1903; Tony Lema, 1964
6 strokes: JH Taylor, 1900; James Braid, 1905; James Braid, 1908; Max Faulkner, 1951; Tom Lehman, 1996; Tiger Woods, 2000; Rory McIlroy, 2014

Champions Who Had Four Rounds, Each Better than the One Before

Jack White, Royal St George's, 1904 – 80, 75, 72, 69
James Braid, Muirfield, 1906 – 77, 76, 74, 73
Ben Hogan, Carnoustie, 1953 – 73, 71, 70, 68
Gary Player, Muirfield, 1959 – 75, 71, 70, 68

Same Number of Strokes in Each of the Four Rounds by a Champion

Denny Shute, St Andrews, 1933 – 73, 73, 73, 73 (excluding the play-off)

Best 18-Hole Recovery by a Champion

George Duncan, Deal, 1920. Duncan was 13 strokes behind the leader, Abe Mitchell, after 36 holes and level with him after 54.

Greatest Variation Between Rounds by a Champion

14 strokes: Henry Cotton, 1934, second round 65, fourth round 79
12 strokes: Henry Cotton, 1934, first round 67, fourth round 79
11 strokes: Jack White, 1904, first round 80, fourth round 69; Greg Norman, 1986, first round 74, second round 63; Greg Norman, 1986, second round 63, third round 74
10 strokes: Seve Ballesteros, 1979, second round 65, third round 75

Greatest Variation Between Two Successive Rounds by a Champion

11 strokes: Greg Norman, 1986, first round 74, second round 63; Greg Norman, 1986, second round 63, third round 74
10 strokes: Seve Ballesteros, 1979, second round 65, third round 75

Greatest Comeback by a Champion

After 18 holes
Harry Vardon, 1896, 11 strokes behind the leader
After 36 holes
George Duncan, 1920, 13 strokes behind the leader
After 54 holes
Paul Lawrie, 1999, 10 strokes behind the leader

Champions Who Had Four Rounds Under 70

Greg Norman, Royal St George's, 1993 – 66, 68, 69, 64; Nick Price, Turnberry, 1994 – 69, 66, 67, 66; Tiger Woods, St Andrews, 2000 – 67, 66, 67, 69; Henrik Stenson, Royal Troon, 2016 – 68, 65, 68, 63; Jordan Spieth, Royal Birkdale, 2017 – 65, 69, 65, 69

Competitors Who Failed to Win The Open Despite Having Four Rounds Under 70

Ernie Els, Royal St George's, 1993 – 68, 69, 69, 68; Jesper Parnevik, Turnberry, 1994 – 68, 66, 68, 67; Ernie Els, Royal Troon, 2004 – 69, 69, 68, 68; Rickie Fowler, Royal Liverpool, 2014 – 69, 69, 68, 67

Lowest Final Round by a Champion

63: Henrik Stenson, Royal Troon, 2016
64: Greg Norman, Royal St George's, 1993
65: Tom Watson, Turnberry, 1977; Seve Ballesteros, Royal Lytham & St Annes, 1988; Justin Leonard, Royal Troon, 1997

Worst Round by a Champion Since 1939

78: Fred Daly, third round, Royal Liverpool, 1947
76: Bobby Locke, second round, Royal St George's, 1949; Paul Lawrie, third round, Carnoustie, 1999

Champion with the Worst Finishing Round Since 1939

75: Sam Snead, St Andrews, 1946

Lowest Opening Round by a Champion

65: Louis Oosthuizen, St Andrews, 2010; Jordan Spieth, Royal Birkdale, 2017

Most Open Championship Appearances

46: Gary Player
43: Sandy Lyle
38: Sandy Herd, Jack Nicklaus, Tom Watson
37: Nick Faldo

Most Final Day Appearances Since 1892

32: Jack Nicklaus
31: Sandy Herd
30: JH Taylor
28: Ted Ray
27: Harry Vardon, James Braid, Nick Faldo
26: Peter Thomson, Gary Player, Tom Watson

Most Appearances by a Champion Before His First Victory

19: Darren Clarke, 2011; Phil Mickelson, 2013
15: Nick Price, 1994
14: Sandy Herd, 1902
13: Ted Ray, 1912; Jack White, 1904; Reg Whitcombe, 1938; Mark O'Meara, 1998
11: George Duncan, 1920; Nick Faldo, 1987; Ernie Els, 2002; Stewart Cink, 2009; Zach Johnson, 2015; Henrik Stenson, 2016

The Open Which Provided the Greatest Number of Rounds Under 70 Since 1946

148 rounds, Turnberry, 1994

The Open with the Fewest Rounds Under 70 Since 1946

2 rounds, St Andrews, 1946; Royal Liverpool, 1947; Carnoustie, 1968

Statistically Most Difficult Hole Since 1982

St Andrews, 1984, Par-4 17th, 4.79

Longest Course in Open History

Carnoustie, 2007, 7,421 yards

Number of Times Each Course Has Hosted The Open

St Andrews, 29; Prestwick, 24; Muirfield, 16; Royal St George's, 14; Royal Liverpool, 12; Royal Lytham & St Annes, 11; Royal Birkdale, 10; Royal Troon, 9; Carnoustie, 8; Musselburgh, 6; Turnberry, 4; Royal Cinque Ports, 2; Royal Portrush, Prince's, 1 each

Increases in Prize Money (£)

Year	Total	First Prize	Year	Total	First Prize	Year	Total	First Prize	Year	Total	First Prize
1860	nil	nil	1890	29.50	13	1966	15,000	2,100	1993	1,000,000	100,000
1863	10	nil	1891	28.50	10	1968	20,000	3,000	1994	1,100,000	110,000
1864	15	6	1892	110	35	1969	30,000	4,250	1995	1,250,000	125,000
1865	20	8	1893	100	30	1970	40,000	5,250	1996	1,400,000	200,000
1866	11	6	1900	125	50	1971	45,000	5,500	1997	1,600,000	250,000
1867	16	7	1910	135	50	1972	50,000	5,500	1998	1,800,000	300,000
1868	12	6	1920	225	75	1975	75,000	7,500	1999	2,000,000	350,000
1872	unknown	8	1927	275	75	1977	100,000	10,000	2000	2,750,000	500,000
1873	unknown	11	1930	400	100	1978	125,000	12,500	2001	3,300,000	600,000
1874	20	8	1931	500	100	1979	155,000	15,000	2002	3,800,000	700,000
1876	27	10	1946	1,000	150	1980	200,000	25,000	2003	3,900,000	700,000
1877	20	8	1949	1,500	300	1982	250,000	32,000	2004	4,000,000	720,000
1878	unknown	8	1951	1,700	300	1983	310,000	40,000	2007	4,200,000	750,000
1879	47	10	1953	2,500	500	1984	451,000	55,000	2010	4,800,000	850,000
1880	unknown	8	1954	3,500	750	1985	530,000	65,000	2011	5,000,000	900,000
1881	21	8	1955	3,750	1,000	1986	600,000	70,000	2013	5,250,000	945,000
1882	47.25	12	1958	4,850	1,000	1987	650,000	75,000	2014	5,400,000	975,000
1883	20	8	1959	5,000	1,000	1988	700,000	80,000	2015	6,300,000	1,150,000
1884	23	8	1960	7,000	1,250	1989	750,000	80,000	2016	6,500,000	1,175,000
1885	35.50	10	1961	8,500	1,400	1990	825,000	85,000	2017	$10,250,000	$1,845,000
1886	20	8	1963	8,500	1,500	1991	900,000	90,000	2018	$10,500,000	$1,890,000
1889	22	8	1965	10,000	1,750	1992	950,000	95,000			

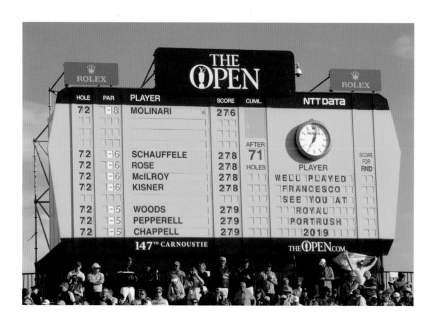

PHOTOGRAPHY CREDITS